THE
LOW-OXALATE
ANTI-INFLAMMATORY
COOKBOOK

THE
LOW-OXALATE
ANTI-INFLAMMATORY
COOKBOOK

75 GLUTEN-FREE, NUT-FREE, SOY-FREE, YEAST-FREE, LOW-SUGAR RECIPES TO HELP YOU STRESS LESS AND FEEL BETTER

CINDY BOKMA

Skyhorse Publishing

Skyhorse Publishing books may be purchased in bulk at special discounts for sales promotion, corporate gifts, fund-raising, or educational purposes. Special editions can also be created to specifications. For details, contact the Special Sales Department, Skyhorse Publishing, 307 West 36th Street, 11th Floor, New York, NY 10018 or info@skyhorsepublishing.com.

Skyhorse® and Skyhorse Publishing® are registered trademarks of Skyhorse Publishing, Inc.®, a Delaware corporation.

Visit our website at www.skyhorsepublishing.com.

10 9 8 7 6 5

Library of Congress Cataloging-in-Publication Data is available on file.

Cover design by Mona Lin

Cover photo by Cindy Bokma

Print ISBN: 978-1-5107-3719-8

Ebook ISBN: 978-1-5107-3721-1

Printed in China

Contents

PART ONE

What You Need to Know

"How is that feeding our bodies has become *more* confusing over the years? Thank goodness for Cindy Bokma, whose own health journey has taken more twists and turns than gluten-free fusilli pasta. After reading her story and devouring her surprisingly comforting recipes, you'll feel clearer in mind, body, and spirit."

—Elizabeth Kendig, Healers Podcast

Introduction

I am not a professional nutritionist or dietician or medical expert. I am also not a chef.

I am however, a home cook who has probably spent more time in the kitchen than any other place. Over the past several years, I have had a myriad of health issues that have been greatly helped by changing the food that I eat.

Ever since I was a little girl paging through my mother's *Good Housekeeping* magazines, I've had an interest in food and health. There is such an undeniable link between what we eat and how we feel, and I'm glad to see more and more people understanding that the food you put into your body directly affects things like mood, skin, energy levels, and so much more. Food has the ability to harm and heal on a deep level.

I like researching and taking notes and understanding wellness, so when my own health began to take a turn, I didn't think twice about finding out what on earth was happening within my own body. For some reason I always want to do things myself and hate asking for help. Going to the doctor is always a last resort if I cannot find out ways to figure out whatever is going wrong.

Several years ago, out of the blue (or so it seemed), I developed a gluten issue. My stomach ached every time I ate cereal, muffins, bread, or pasta, which was at least a few times a week. The talk of gluten was everywhere from the health blogs to magazine articles. With all of that in mind, I decided to remove gluten from my diet to see if I felt better—and I never turned back. However, I don't recommend eliminating gluten before getting tested, as it makes a firm diagnosis difficult.

Since I had gone off gluten, the tests to see if I had celiac were inconclusive. Going back on gluten for six weeks would likely give me a definite answer, but I didn't want to be sick for over a month. I highly recommend getting tested if you think you have celiac or a gluten intolerance.

Diving into gluten-free cooking, I armed myself with almond flour cookies and spinach smoothies, I ate gluten-free toast with peanut butter every morning with a handful of almonds in between meals. Black, pinto, or kidney beans in chili or taco salad was something I made often, and hummus was one of my favorite snacks. I used tahini in my chocolate chip cookies, baked scones, and Irish soda bread with almond flour as gluten-free and paleo cookbooks directed me to do.

Then my interstitial cystitis (IC) began to act up. IC is a condition commonly known as "painful bladder disease" and presents the same symptoms as a bladder infection. If you have ever suffered from a bladder infection, you know about the pain and discomfort.

It was so bad that I was up going to the bathroom at least twenty times a night. The next day I'd barely function from lack of sleep, I'd also be highly irritable because I was so exhausted. I tried many supplements, but found little relief. With two kids who needed me, I was lucky if I made it through the day without a nap. My doctor put me on a medication that was over two hundred dollars for a single bottle to last the month. I used the medication sparingly, choosing to suffer instead. I had guilt over spending so much money on the prescription.

I joined message boards and asked questions, praying for something, somewhere to help. When a member asked if I had been watching my oxalates, I had no idea what she was talking about.

Oxalates?

No, I was a healthy eater. I made all of my own food. I was paleo! I was gluten-free! I made green smoothies every day and sprinkled chia seeds on my yogurt!

At the time I didn't bother to research oxalates, dismissing them just as I had skipped over the topic of pyroluria and high histamines (more on this in a little bit!). No, I was so healthy with all my almond flour muffins and peanut butter protein cookies, there was no way I had any other issues besides the gluten thing and the IC.

Things were so bad however that whenever my family went anywhere, I'd have to make sure bathrooms were easily available, basing activities on whether or not I could reach a restroom. Think about that for second: my day was planned around the location of bathrooms—especially on vacations.

A cruise around Seattle? Great, would there be bathrooms?

A tour of a glacier? Okay, but is there a restroom?

A long drive up the coast? Only if we can stop frequently for potty breaks!

I'll never forget being in Alaska and wanting to do a horseback riding excursion, but I couldn't because . . . what if I had to pee? I also remember my husband driving around on vacation trying to find a health food store looking for specific supplements, anything to help me with the extreme discomfort I was experiencing.

Maybe I should look into those oxalates.

The very basic description is that oxalates are kind of like a built-in pesticide in vegetables, fruits, nuts, and seeds, acting as a deterrent for insects and other small pests. We cannot digest oxalates; they are usually moved through the digestive tract and eliminated. For people with

"leaky gut syndrome," however, this is where oxalates become a problem.

Leaky gut is when the junctures of the gut are not tight as they should be, allowing food particles, bacteria, and toxins to slip through. Kind of like a tightly knit sweater where the yarn becomes loose and holes emerge. You might see leaky gut referred to as intestinal permeability. Signs include bloating, gas, cramping, fatigue, joint pain, and rashes.

It's linked to inflammation, and autoimmune diseases like chronic fatigue, rheumatoid arthritis, lupus, and leaky gut can trigger other illnesses. If you think this sounds serious, you're right.

It is possible for oxalates to act as a poison if the diet does not contain enough calcium. Calcium binds with oxalates and helps keep it from being absorbed. Most people, like those without any food sensitivities or leaky gut, are able to consume and break down oxalates without a problem. When overaccumulation of oxalates occur, it becomes an issue for our kidneys, and oxalates are not properly flushed out. Our livers also make small amounts of oxalates.

Oxalate crystals are often found in kidney stones (this is the most well-known oxalate-related condition) yet they can also make themselves at home in your joints, bones, lungs, nerve tissues, eyes, thyroid, and brain.

I was shocked when I found that oxalates are in fruits and vegetables, nuts and legumes. Nearly everything I consumed on a daily basis was extremely high in oxalates! Could there be a link between my bladder pain, headaches, blurry vision, and oxalates?

As I studied up this topic, I came to the sinking conclusion that I had completely overdone my oxalate intake and was dismayed to think I'd have to remove these foods from my diet.

Wasn't going gluten-free enough? Every time I had something containing high oxalates, I'd experience severe bladder pain and frequency and the whole sleep-irritability-fatigue-headache cycle would happen all over again.

It was clear to me that I was overdoing it, and I couldn't help but wonder about other people who were doing the same. People with kidney stones are often advised to watch their oxalates, but what about people like me who didn't have kidney stones, but presented a clear problem with oxalate intake?

Most of the cookbooks I used called for almond flour as an ingredient to bake with or use in various recipes, especially baking and frequently a substitute for breading. The majority of my gluten-free cookbooks called for other favorites such as sweet potatoes, black beans, celery, dates to sweeten baked goods, grains like brown rice, kamut, and amaranth, plus sesame seeds, and a liberal use of green tea and turmeric.

The more I read about oxalates, the more I realized my body couldn't process these even in small amounts.

Though I lowered my oxalate intake, I still had headaches, blurry vision, and felt generally exhausted from the time I got up in the morning until I went to bed.

I went to several alternative medical professionals including a Chinese medicine doctor, acupuncturist, a reiki practitioner, a holistic health doctor, my general physician, and a urologist, and no one could accurately figure out what was wrong until I saw an integrative medical doctor who ordered a barrage of tests and concluded I had systemic candida.

Another piece of my health puzzle slipped into place. In addition to going gluten-free and watching oxalates, I was now instructed to not consume any sugar and go low carb.

At the time I was also diagnosed with adrenal fatigue. There was so much going on inside my body, I didn't know what to do. What on earth could I eat to help my body heal?

Turning to vegan recipes, I found that cashews and cashew milk are frequent replacements for dairy products, which doesn't work for people like me who have a nut allergy. Many vegetarian options called for other high-oxalate foods. The healthiest of cookbooks used high-oxalate ingredients plus a constant call for almond flour.

I grew frustrated. I felt like I couldn't eat anything! I was trying to plan meals for my family that were low-carb, no sugar, gluten-free, no yeast, no soy, no nuts, no legumes, and low-oxalate. It seemed like all I could eat was white rice, and later I discovered the white rice was feeding the candida, so I couldn't even eat that!

Health is a like a line of dominoes and once one falls, others soon follow. A leaky gut can lead to candida, which complicates oxalate issues, leading to bladder issues, leading to sleepless nights. Lack of rest results in stress, which ends with adrenal fatigue, which leads to pyroluria, a condition where the body lacks B vitamins and zinc. That diagnosis led to me to find that I also had high histamine levels, which manifest in things like headaches, anxiety, rapid heartbeat, cramps, fatigue, and more.

From the bladder condition to the adrenal fatigue to the pyroluria and candida and high histamines, I was certain I would never eat like a normal person again.

From the hundreds of hours of reading on the topic of oxalates, I have seen several conditions linked, and I hope that my own health journey can inspire others to delve into research and discovering information that can help. There is so much out there, and new information comes up very often.

Chapter 1

About Oxalates

Though I felt better on a gluten-free, low-oxalate diet, I kept investigating, surprised at how many health issues were impacted by oxalates. Surely I wasn't the only person suffering from an inability to consume them, was I? You know how when you are suffering, you feel like the only person in the world with that problem? Going out to eat or over to someone's house for dinner created so much stress for me that I would end up staying home or eating before I left the house.

If you have a leaky gut, chances are more oxalates are slipping through your intestines because the junctions in your gut aren't tight enough to keep them out. And while most people can freely consume foods with oxalates, it's those of us who have underlying health issues, like candida or leaky gut, who suffer the most.

Our guts need healthy bacteria to break down oxalates. If our intestines are not functioning properly, we may not have the ability to break down oxalates. I was listening to a podcast recently about Small Intestine Bacterial Overgrowth (SIBO) and the health specialist mentioned how many people lack the proper enzymes to break down oxalates thanks to the chemicals sprayed on our foods and the fact that many people eat processed foods, which our bodies were not designed to break down. It was a theory that made sense to me.

I can't help but wonder if oxalates will be the new gluten. Learning about oxalates was like entering into a new world. I'm trying to give you the broad scope on this topic, but there are many details that are complex and scientific.

Not a whole lot of people are connecting the dots from healthy foods to health problems. And why would they? We try to eat foods recommended by experts but what happens when you don't get better or end up feeling worse?

Recently I chatted with a friend who suffered from a myriad of symptoms and was tested by doctors who couldn't find a diagnosis. They ended up giving her painkillers. There was absolutely no discussion of what she ate, no talk of oxalates. After we went over what she was eating on a daily basis, we found out her diet was extremely high in oxalates, and she began to decrease her oxalate consumption, feeling better within a few days.

When oxalates are not broken down and flushed out, they can be stored all over the body and affect the organs. It's not surprising excess oxalates cause inflammation. There is research available about the illness-oxalate connection but you have to put on your thinking cap and dive in pretty deep.

In order to help with inflammation, I began taking turmeric, only to discover that turmeric is high in oxalates! The supplements I took for my anxiety made me feel worse, not better, and when I checked out the oxalate content? You might have guessed, high in oxalates.

Many doctors may not be familiar with oxalates and miss the connection to health issues. I visited a urogynecologist for the IC and holistic practitioner for stomachaches, trying to get to the root of my problems, and neither brought up oxalates. Yet on both an IC message board and a high-histamine message board, numerous people noted a link between oxalates and bladder issues and when reducing oxalates, a noticeable change is seen.

Low energy, weakness, brain fog, burning sensation in feet, headaches, genital irritation, joint and muscle pain, as well as intestinal pain are all linked to high oxalate consumption. Mood can also be affected by oxalates, causing anxiety, lack of sleep, and depression.

Conditions linked to high oxalates include asthma, autism, thyroid-related illness, chronic fatigue, fibromyalgia, inflammatory bowel disease, interstitial cystitis, kidney stones, headaches—including migraines—seizures, and vulvodynia.

Oxalates can contribute to Hashimoto's and other thyroid conditions and I have read about a relationship between oxalates and celiac disease. I recently read that there is a link between chronic candida and oxalates. At the end of this book, I list resources for further reading regarding oxalates. I encourage you to do research and learn from the experts like Susan Owens, whose knowledge about oxalates is awe-inspiring. The topic gets incredibly scientific and detailed.

As I continued to seek answers and find food I could safely eat, I discovered cookbooks that addressed gluten intolerances often called for almond flour as well as other high-oxalate ingredients.

I was and still am, dismayed to see many Paleo, plant-based, and gluten-free cookbooks include almond flour, high-oxalate vegetables, and cashew or almond milk. In fact, I get excited reading new recipes from some amazing Paleo chefs on Instagram, but am typically let down when they use almond flour again and again in their baked goods. I want to scream about oxalates!

Cookbooks for vegans include nut products especially cashews, and high-oxalate vegetables, plus legumes as staples. Cookbooks that address leaky gut often do not include recipes that are low in oxalates. They might be out there but I haven't seen any including low-oxalate options.

My goal with this cookbook is to revamp some of my favorite recipes and create new ones to be gluten-free, low-oxalate, low-sugar, no nuts, yeast-free, soy-free, and suitable (and helpful) for anyone dealing with a very limited diet, which can be extremely overwhelming. Yes, I have cried real tears out of frustration for the foods I can no longer eat! If this describes you, I understand!

Boiling causes oxalates to "leak" out and can help reduce soluble oxalate by more than 60 percent. Steaming is another option for high-oxalate vegetables such as carrots, Swiss chard, and spinach. I like boiling best, and when I make my seasoned carrots, I always boil them before roasting them in the oven to remove some oxalates. Be sure to throw out the cooking water. Whether you boil, bake, or steam your vegetables, nothing will completely get rid of oxalates.

With great success, I have used a product called Nephure. It's made using an enzyme from blue-green algae that you add to water and drink after consuming oxalates. It helps me after consuming high-oxalate treats like peanut butter or French fries.

I encourage you to keep a food diary and make note of any stomachaches, headaches, cramping, bladder pain, or anxiety after eating various foods. For the longest time I kept a list of high-oxalate vegetables and fruits with me when I went grocery shopping so I wouldn't accidentally purchase something high-oxalate.

Though I cannot tolerate consuming most high-oxalate foods and foods containing histamines, I can eat tomatoes once in a while without a problem. Bacon is high in histamines, but I eat a little without experiencing bladder pain, yet spinach and peanut butter send me into a flare of symptoms. Everyone is bioindividual, which is why it's so important to pay attention to how you feel after eating.

Soluble and Insoluble Oxalates

Soluble oxalates go through the intestinal barrier, while insoluble oxalates are not as easily absorbed, but those with leaky gut like me will end up absorbing more of the insoluble oxalates. Everyone has different abilities to break down oxalates, so there is no one-size-fits-all way to handle consuming foods with oxalates though I try to avoid anything very high oxalates and if I cannot resist a piece of chocolate, I know I need to pay attention to whatever else I am eating over the next few days.

Chapter 2

High- and Low-Oxalate Foods

I love spinach and sweet potatoes, and consumed them daily before learning about oxalates. I'm embarrassed to tell you how much I baked with almond flour. Looking back, I think I was consuming the equivalent of 90 almonds in one sitting as I enjoyed my almond-flour scones and cookies. I wonder how many people are consuming oxalates like I was?

High-Oxalate Foods	Low to Medium-Oxalate Fruits	Low-Oxalate Vegetables
Spinach	Apples	Avocado
Tofu	Apricots (lower medium)	Banana pepper
Chocolate	Cantaloupe	Fresh basil
Rhubarb	Cherries (medium dried)	Bok choy
Swiss chard	Cranberries (fresh are low but dried are medium)	Broccoli
Beets	Dates; these vary but Medjools are low	Cabbage
Peanuts		Cauliflower
Almonds	Fresh fig (varies from medium to high)	Carrots, boiled
Sweet potatoes		Chives
Legumes	Green and red grapes	Cucumber
Wheat bran	Lemon can vary; some are high, so use cautiously	Garlic
Buckwheat		Mushrooms
Amaranth	Mango	Onions
	Oranges can vary; some are high, so use cautiously	Snow peas
		Snow peas (medium)
	Peaches	Sweet bell peppers (orange, green, and yellow are medium unless miniatures)
	Golden raisins (sultana and dark raisins, like golden raisins, are low per ¼ cup, medium if more than that)	Radishes
		Shallots
		Yellow squash
	Watermelon	Butternut squash
		Water chestnuts
		Zucchini

Medium-Oxalate Vegetables

Artichoke

Eggplant

Belgian Endive

Jicama

Curly Kale

Leeks (raw)

Tomatoes (some varieties) most are medium and roma/plums are high

★ Take into consideration that many different varieties of the same fruits/vegetable can have different oxalate contents. For example, ½ cup of Big Beef or Brandywine tomatoes are low ox while ½ cup of Beefmaster, Better Boy, Carolina Gold, Celebrity, Early Girl Valencia are medium ox.

Low-Oxalate Seeds/Nuts/Grains

Chestnuts

Flax Seeds

Pumpkin Seeds (I buy the sprouted pumpkin seeds)

Macadamia Nuts

Red Lentils

White Rice

Cellophane Noodles

Low-Oxalate Spices and Condiments

Almond extract

Basil

Capers

Chives

Cilantro

Dill

Ginger (fresh, not dried)

Marjoram

Mustard

Nutmeg is medium, mace (from the same plant) is very low

Parsley

White pepper

Rosemary

Saffron

Sage

Savory

Tarragon

Thyme

Vanilla extract

Horseradish

Ketchup

Mayonnaise

Dijon mustard

Vinegar

Low-Oxalate Spice Combinations

Try experimenting with adding your own spices to the recipes in this book. Here are a few of my favorite spice combinations.

basil, garlic, onion, oregano

cumin, garlic, chili (cumin is very high, I use sparingly, and the chili varies)

cloves, garlic, ginger (cloves and dried ginger are very high, I use very sparingly)

oregano, rosemary, thyme, basil

herbs de provence, thyme, garlic powder, rosemary

cardamom, cloves, ginger (cloves and dried ginger are very high, cardamom is medium)

Himalayan sea salt, white pepper, garlic powder, onion powder

Low-Oxalate Baking

Agave Nectar

Almond Extract

White Chocolate

Baking Soda

Cornstarch

Rice Starch

Stevia extract (Sweet Leaf); stevia powder is very low as well

Low-Oxalate Breads/ Grains

Plain Tortillas, Udi's brand

Corn and Rice Chex

½ cup gluten-free Black Rice noodles, King Soba

½ cup gluten-free cellophane noodles

½ cup gluten-free brown rice elbow noodles, Tinkyada

½ cup gluten-free white rice spaghetti, Tinkyada

½ cup gluten-free rice noodles from Thai Kitchen

½ cup white rice

Medium-Oxalate Bread

Udi's gluten-free hamburger bun

Kinnikinnick Tapioca Rice hamburger bun

Udi's white sandwich bread

Low-Oxalate Flours

(all gluten-free, ¼–½ cup tested unless otherwise noted)

Bob's Red Mill Flaxseed Meal Flour (1 tablespoon)

Bob's Red Mill Coconut Flour

Cowpea Bean Flour (Black Eyed Pea)

Garbanzo Bean Flour

Bob's Red Mill Potato Starch

Rice Starch

Barry Farms Sweet Potato Flour

Authentic Foods Rice Flour, superfine

Betty Crocker gluten-free pizza crust mix

Betty Crocker All-Purpose Rice Floor Blend

Southern Glory Biscuit Mix (gluten-free)

Medium-Oxalate Flours

(all gluten-free, ¼–½ cup tested)

Expendex Modified Tapicoa Starch

Bobs Red Mill Malted Barley flour

High Rock Farm Chestnut flour

WEDO Green Banana flour

NOW White Rice Flour

Bob's Red Mill Brown Rice Flour

Arrowhead Mills Brown Rice Flour

Gemini Tigernut Flour

Mama's Coconut Flour Blend

Pamela's All-Purpose Artisan Blend, Non-Dairy

Krusteaz All-Purpose Flour

Chapter 3

Histamines

A Quick Word About Histamines and Oxalates

I'm certain that a lifetime of worry and anxiety has contributed to a leaky gut, which has led to my health issues and an inability to break down certain foods. I remember being a little girl in elementary school and clutching my stomach in pain every time I got nervous or worried, which was often.

Recently I discovered the role of histamines in foods, discovering that oxalates release histamines. This might be a worthwhile topic to research if you find that you are sensitive to foods such as cured meats, yogurt, kombucha, vinegar, and wine.

Once I started paying attention to my symptoms and what I was eating beyond oxalates, I discovered histamines were affecting me too. I had blood work done to validate my suspicions and I had super high histamine levels.

Histamines are chemicals in the body and they are involved with the immune system, digestion, and the central nervous system. When histamines are released, they begin to flood the body via the bloodstream and an inflammatory response occurs.

High histamine levels are caused by a few different issues: allergies, Small Intestine Bacterial Overgrowth (SIBO), leaky gut, a lack of diamine oxidase (the enzyme that breaks down histamines), and consuming histamine-rich foods.

There is a histamine-oxalate link; oxalates release histamines in the body. I am new to learning about histamines but wanted to include this information in case you are carefully monitoring what you are eating and don't see the relief you are looking for after going low-oxalate.

High-histamine foods include:

avocados

bacon, salami, and pepperoni

bananas

canned, cured, or dried meats

canned, marinated, or dried fish

cheeses

cocoa and carob

dried fruit

eggplant

guava

kiwi

kombucha

lemons

lentils, beans, and soy/soy products

oranges

papaya

pears

pickles and pickled vegetables

pineapples

raspberries

sauerkraut

smoked fish

spinach

strawberries

vinegar

walnuts, cashews, and peanuts

wine and beer

yogurt

In this cookbook, I do feature bacon, kielbasa, avocado, strawberries, and cheese; these are ingredients I don't eat often and use sparingly. I know if I eat these a few days in a row I will need to take some supplements to help break down the histamines.

As with the oxalates, take notes on how you feel after eating certain foods so you can determine what is affecting your health.

Chapter 4

Inflammatory Ingredients

The word "inflammation" literally means "set afire" so you can imagine your body red, swollen, and painful on the inside. Chronic inflammation leads to disease, which is what we want to avoid, our goal being to have excellent physical and mental health.

Inflammatory foods can increase the chance of obesity, heart disease, and diabetes, as well as chronic diseases like Alzheimer's disease, rheumatoid arthritis, lupus, and Crohn's disease, just to name a few.

Top Inflammatory Foods/Ingredients

Sugar	Saturated Fats
Vegetable-Oil	Margarine/shortening
Fried Foods	Refined Grains
Refined Flour	Yeast
Dairy	MSG
Artificial Sweeteners	Gluten
Artificial Additives	Alcohol

Let's take a closer look at some of the most popular inflammatory ingredients.

SUGAR

Growing up, my mother wouldn't buy those sugary cereals that looked so enticing with colors not found in nature. We'd always had the super-low-sugar, healthy cereals that I found so unexciting. Bran? Oats? How about orange and pink marshmallows or chocolate chips?

When I lived on my own, I bought those sugar-saturated cereals that I had been dreaming about my whole life, and found that, yes, they were delicious, but I didn't get a sugar rush or have energy after eating a bowl of fruity cereal; rather, I felt depressed and sluggish. My skin broke out and eventually I grew nauseated at the sight of them. At the restaurant where I worked, I ate butter mints when I was bored or hungry and noticed the same pattern of feeling exhausted and barely able to keep my eyes open. The link between sugar and my energy level was obvious.

I didn't completely avoid white sugar until fairly recently. Now that I know how sugar affects health, I see it's one of the worst things you can consume.

White sugar/high fructose corn syrup has been proven to lead to cancer, obesity, insulin resistance, diabetes, and fatty liver disease. The only sugars I like are coconut sugar and the natural sugars found in fruit. When I bake, I use coconut sugar, and if I'm making a cake I will use organic, raw white sugar and typically I decrease the sugar.

Sugar is a major factor in obesity and heart disease and is more addictive than drugs. Those sugary cereals I wanted so badly are just empty calories, filling you up with zero nutritional content and robbing your body of vitamins and minerals.

While I avoid white sugar in my day-to-day life, I bake with organic sugar occasionally and don't deny myself a treat now and then. Everything in moderation is my motto.

VEGETABLE OIL + MARGARINE

Unlike butter, ghee, olive oil, or coconut oil, which are pure, vegetable oils (such as corn, grapeseed, peanut, sunflower, canola, plus margarine and shortening) undergo a chemical process using petroleum solvent.

Before the chemical process, the oil is dark and dirty looking. In order for it to be cleaned and deodorized, it's put through a series of steps.

The oil is filtered, bleached, and deodorized to remove any harsh scents and more chemicals are added to change the color and even more chemicals are mixed in to stabilize the oils so they have a longer shelf life. What are left behind from the original oil are trans fatty acids.

Sounds good, right?

MedicineNet.com describes it like this:

> Trans fatty acid: An unhealthy substance that is made through the chemical process of hydrogenation of oils. Hydrogenation solidifies liquid oils and increases the shelf life and the flavor stability of oils and foods that contain them. Trans fatty acids are found in vegetable shortening and in some margarine, crackers, cookies, and snack foods. Trans fatty acids are also found in abundance in many deep-fried foods.

The trans fatty acids raise the LDL cholesterol levels (this is the "bad" kind of cholesterol) which build up in the walls of the arteries, and it lowers the HDL ("good") cholesterol. Natural fats are better for you than the chemically produced oils and margarines.

GLUTEN

There's so much to be said about gluten. Growing up, gluten wasn't a word we all knew like we do now. When I began having my stomach problems, I only knew about gluten because it was the hottest buzzword. I had no clue that gluten can damage the lining of the intestines, causing leaky gut, or that it could trigger inflammation.

Saying I was gluten-free reminded me of the "fat-free" craze when I'd eat an entire coffee cake because it was "fat free" and I wouldn't worry past the fat part. Gluten, however, is not just a craze or a fad. Those suffering from celiac and other autoimmune disorders have a very serious reason to stay away from gluten. It can be extremely toxic.

The Celiac Disease Foundation describes gluten like this:

> Gluten is a general name for the proteins found in wheat (wheatberries, durum, emmer, semolina, spelt, farina, farro, graham, KAMUT® khorasan wheat and einkorn), rye, barley and triticale—a cross between wheat and rye. Gluten helps foods maintain their shape, acting as glue that holds food together. Gluten can be found in many types of foods, even ones that would not be expected.

Gluten can act as an irritant for many people, causing inflammatory responses like stomach pains, diarrhea, cramping, bloating. There are many symptoms of gluten sensitivity that range from headaches to mood issues to canker sores and rashes. There's even a link between gluten and depression, anxiety, and schizophrenia which shows this little protein can be toxic in ways that we don't expect.

When I was heavily researching my symptoms, gluten came up again and again.

I grew up in New Jersey eating bagels and pizza and pasta. Stopping for a bagel after school was something I did all the time with no stomach problems other than a little bloating. So what changed between then and now? Today's wheat contains more herbicides which contain the active ingredient glyphosate. Glyphosate has been steadily used over the past fifteen years. It disrupts the beneficial bacteria in our guts, leading to leaky gut which then leads to all kinds of inflammatory health issues.

One of the doctors I consulted with while I was trying to figure out what was wrong with my stomach told me that many people are actually reacting not so much to the gluten, but to the glyphosates. Either way, I avoid gluten and encourage you to research the gluten-glyphosate-leaky gut connection and decide for yourself.

ARTIFICAL SWEETENER

I guess the 1980s were a really interesting time to grow up because not only did us eighties kids get to enjoy everything chemically manufactured to be fat-free, but we also were among the first to chew sugar-free gum made with artificial sweeteners.

I've always liked chewing gum, I don't know why—maybe it's my introverted, nervous nature. As soon as a certain brand of gum hit the shelves I made sure I was always fully stocked with a pack or two in my Jansport backpack. So what if the warning on the label spelled out that the chemicals were shown to cause cancer in rats? Surely the rats were given huge amounts of NutraSweet (a.k.a. aspartame), not the tiny bit in the gum I was chewing.

While I liked the gum, what I didn't like was giant cystic acne I was getting along my jawline. When I didn't chew this particular gum, I didn't get the deep pimples. As soon as I chewed so much as one piece, a pimple would surface, subterranean and painful. Finally, I stopped chewing that particular gum. The cystic acne only came back whenever I consumed an artificial sweetener, which by now is pretty much never.

In reading about reactions to artificial sweeteners, I've found people have the following reactions: headaches, migraines, dizziness, seizures, rashes, weight gain, joint pain, and fatigue among other things. Ongoing consumption of artificial sweeteners leads to chronic inflammation which leads to a worsening of symptoms pertaining to diabetes, Alzheimer's disease, Parkinson's disease, and chronic fatigue.

In reading about aspartame, I have yet to see a connection to the cystic acne I experienced but that is the link I determined. You may experience other weird symptoms. It's worth noting if you see a connection. Artificial sweeteners are found a lot in gum and diet soda, and they are also used in processed foods.

These low-calorie sweet substances also go by the names saccharin, acesulfame, neotame, and sucralose as well as the one I mentioned, aspartame. Over six thousand products contain artificial sweeteners, such as yogurt, breath mints, candies, gum, alcohol, diet drinks, and even medication. NutraSweet, Equal, Splenda, and Sweet N' Low are some of the names you probably recognize.

Some immune systems (like mine, I am sensitive from head to toe) will attack the "foreign invader" aka chemical sweetener, and trigger inflammation. They may also produce carcinogenic effects.

MSG

MSG/Monosodium glutamate is a sneaky food additive that goes by many names, so you really have to know how to read a label. You could see it listed as any of the following:

Textured protein

Autolyzed yeast

Yeast extract

Yeast food

Glutamate

Glutamic Acid

Autolyzed plant protein

Sodium caseinate

Calcium caseinate

Hydrolyzed protein

Hydrolyzed vegetable protein (HVP)

Hydrolyzed plant protein (HPP)

Soy protein extract

Natural flavors

MSG is found in processed foods like drinks, soups, dry soup mixes, cold cuts, seasoning salt, dressings, chips, fast foods, and frozen dinners. A staggering 95 percent of processed foods contain MSG.

It's considered to be an "excitotoxin," which are a group of amino acids that overexcite the neurons in the brain, leading to cell death. MSG is often used because it makes food tastier and gives pep to bland foods.

Consumption of MSG has been associated with autism, diabetes, liver inflammation, obesity, and even ADHD. Common allergic reactions include headaches, nausea, heart palpitations. There are countless articles discussing the health risks of heavy intake of MSG. Your best bet is to cook for yourself and skip processed foods. My own rule is that anything out of a drive-thru, a box, a bag, or a can is to be used sparingly.

Chapter 5

In the Kitchen

Kitchen Tools

When you are cooking every day, there are some items that will make your life a lot easier. I use the following constantly and recommend having them in your kitchen so prep work is quick and efficient.

I have everything I need within easy reach: pots and pans near the stovetop, spoons and utensils in a container next to the stove, and sheet pans and pizza pans, as well as potholders, next to the oven.

Salad Spinner

When buying organic lettuce, I've noticed that it's not always clean and free of dirt. I've even found little bugs hidden within the leaves of organic lettuce.

I always wash lettuce thoroughly, then set it in the salad spinner and give it a whirl. I then spread the lettuce leaves out on paper towels to dry completely.

I also use my salad spinner for fresh herbs, cleaning and drying them and then wrapping them in a paper towel and storing in a ziplock baggie.

Food Processor

How did I ever make it through life without one of these? Not only is a food processor a must-have for chopping, dicing, or slicing, but I use it to blend smoothies and soups. I probably use my food processor most to make cauliflower rice.

You can also grind meats, seeds, and nuts, make bread crumbs, and more. It's such a versatile tool to have in the kitchen and you can buy one for around $25. Mine is a basic model, but it gets the job done.

Blender

I invested in the best blender I could find and got a Vitamix. I absolutely love it. This high-powered blender is used to mince, shred, and chop vegetables, and break down frozen fruit and ice. It emulsifies liquids and quickly purees. Blenders are also good at pulverizing larger ingredients.

I use this when I need to liquefy a larger volume of ingredients and keep the food processor for chopping and dicing.

Spiralizer

I bought my spiralizer specifically for making zucchini noodles. It reminds me of a huge pencil sharpener and is used by placing the fruit or vegetable in a clamp then turning a handle.

You can get really creative with the spiralizer, and everything looks so pretty piled into long ribbons. I've seen people using their spiralizer for a wide variety of cool veggie ribbons, but I use mine for zoodles!

Crock-Pot

The Crock-Pot is one of the best investments you can make for the kitchen. Throw some ingredients in there and, hours later, come back to a finished meal. I've found that most meats cook best over a long period of time at a lower setting. Cooking in the Crock-Pot ensures your food will cook at a consistent pace. I've made corned beef and roast in the Crock-Pot and both turned out very tender.

Meats and vegetables simmer in their own juices, and you don't need a lot of oil or butter.

My most used recipe for the Crock-Pot is to place chicken breasts, a little oil, and some chopped vegetables along with dried spices (fresh spices and herbs will go limp) and turn the Crock-Pot on low. I check after a few hours to see the progress of whatever is inside.

The kitchen smells so good whenever the Crock-Pot is on! Making bone broth in the Crock-Pot, set on low for a good twenty-four hours, is something I do very often. Soups and stews are ideal to make in the Crock-Pot. You can also throw together a casserole, meatballs, pulled pork, applesauce, and so much more.

Immersion Blender

You might also see immersion blenders called wand or stick blenders but no matter what the name, this is a tool I keep close by for various mixing needs. It takes up little space and is easy to clean. It's also relatively inexpensive.

An immersion blender is ideal when you don't want to lug out the food processor or blender. This tool is what I use for my Cauliflower Soup and salad dressings.

Salsa, sauces, pesto, and egg whites can all be mixed and blended using this nifty tool. It can't create a smoothie from frozen fruit (at least mine can't) or knead dough, but for smaller, simpler jobs, it's perfect. It also gets the lumps out of gravy, pancake batter, and milkshakes.

Cutting Boards

I have a small variety of cutting boards for even the tiniest of jobs. I want to protect my countertops, and always use something underneath whatever it is I'm cutting. Plastic is my first choice, though it can harbor bacteria from poultry, so be sure to always thoroughly clean the boards.

I do not use the same cutting board for meats or poultry as I do for vegetables and fruits. Though I do use mostly plastic, I also like wood cutting boards.

Knives

A good set of knives is another must-have. Invest in some decent knives because these will be your most used tools in the kitchen besides spoons.

I have several knives of different shapes and sizes but two are my favorites; one is a small-medium super sharp paring knife that works to peel, slice, trim, cut, and chop vegetables/fruits. I also like a serrated knife for cutting fruits and vegetables with smooth skin. The jagged edge of the knife enables me to cut through the soft skin of a tomato or equally squishy soft fruits and vegetables. Typically the serrated knives are used for breads, but I also use mine to cut up produce.

Skillet with a Lid

I use my skillet all the time, and when I want something to cook slowly, I put the lid on it and turn the flame to low. My favorite skillet is large enough to fit four hamburgers and deep enough to make a one-pan dish.

Mixing Bowls

I have a set of glass mixing bowls that include small, medium, large, and extra-large bowls.

These are great for mixing various ingredients when I bake or even storing leftovers.

I use the extra-large bowl for parties and use it for chips. You can't go wrong with a set of glass mixing bowls.

Measuring Cups

I have both individual measuring cups and a large glass measuring cup. The smaller ones are nice to have for the little things I have to measure, such as a single cup of flour or a quarter cup of coconut sugar, and I like the larger glass one for liquids like broth or water. I like having several options especially when you are doing a lot of cooking and need to use the measuring cups for different things.

I have stainless steel measuring cups that I use to measure rice or dry ingredients.

Utensils

In my kitchen I have a small variety of utensils that I use for different tasks, the turner spatulas are for scrambling eggs and cooking meat or poultry in the skillet while the wooden spoons are used for things like pasta and rice.

I use my vegetable peeler to remove the skins from cucumbers, carrots and other vegetables that require the skin removed. A whisk is nice to have on hand for sauces and gravy while a ladle is your best bet for serving soup into bowls. A slotted spoon will help drain foods like pasta and rice.

Bakeware

If you bake breads or coffee cakes, it's a good idea to have some quality bakeware. My favorite is glass. I frequently use my 8 by 8-inch glass pan as well as a 9 by 13-inch baking pan, and a pizza pan, cookie/baking sheets, and various sized glassware to reheat leftovers. I prefer glass over anything else because it is so durable and long lasting.

You can find surprisingly nice kitchen tools at places like HomeGoods, Marshalls, and TJ Maxx. I have purchased a lot of my kitchen tools from them, and have ordered larger kitchen items from Amazon. I bought my blender directly from Vitamix. Costco offers good small appliances as well.

Chapter 6

About the Recipes in this Book + Tips

Most recipes are based on servings for a family of four. Depending on how much you or your family eats, you may have more or less left over. I always like leftover chicken for salads, and I keep a little ground beef for extra tacos or to throw in scrambled eggs for extra protein.

Feel free to experiment with the spices, especially salt, garlic, and white pepper. I tend to like more salt and garlic powder. The recipes in this book typically feature a conservative amount of spices; keep adding spices by the ½ teaspoon and taste frequently to adjust to your liking. I keep several wooden spoons in a jar next to the stovetop just for tasting!

Don't be afraid to add more, less, or even different spices and herbs. Make notes as you go along and determine what tastes good according to your palate. My recipes are guides for low-oxalate eating, but you will probably want to adjust ingredients depending on your tastes.

Fine-tune the seasonings to your preferences so you enjoy the recipes! Having to be low-oxalate can be a challenge, but I want the cooking process to be easy and fun for you.

I try to cook within a half an hour, so most of the main dishes will require a time commitment of 30 to 40 minutes from start to finish. Cleaning up as I cook helps the process move along, and if I know I'm going to need to do something that takes time, like boiling water or preheating the oven, that's something I will begin as soon as I step into the kitchen.

Please note: A few of the recipes contain medium-oxalate ingredients. I make note when something isn't very low or low-oxalate so you can determine if it's a food you may or may not be able to tolerate. Tomatoes, green beans, carrots, paprika, French fries, and certain flour blends I use are medium-oxalate.

Boiling helps in reducing soluble oxalate content by 30 to 87 percent and boiling significantly reduces both soluble and insoluble oxalate contents. However, boiling may decrease the amount of nutrients in the vegetables.

I give you as much information as I have discovered in my research but always encourage you to get online and research for yourself.

GROCERY SHOPPING

I try to buy organic when it makes sense. For example, if regular apples are $1.29 a pound and organic is only ten cents more, I will buy organic. I try to shop within a budget and make healthy choices for my family by skipping the chips, candy, and sugary cereals.

I shop at Trader Joe's frequently because they offer a good selection of organic items plus affordable gluten-free foods and great spices. I also shop at local market called Sprouts, and we buy bulk organic beef and chicken from Costco, I'm happy that Costco offers so many organic products.

Ingredients that I always have on hand:

From these you can usually throw something together for a meal, even at the very last minute.

Protein:

Ground beef
Chicken breasts
Ground turkey
No-nitrate bacon

Baking:

Organic coconut flour
Bob's Red Mill Gluten-Free 1-to-1 Baking Flour (sweet white rice flour, whole grain brown rice flour, potato starch, whole grain sweet white sorghum flour, tapioca flour, xanthan gum)
Mama's Coconut Flour Blend (white rice flour, tapioca flour, potato starch, organic coconut flour, sweet rice flour) *medium oxalate
Baking powder
Baking soda
Xanthan gum
Gluten-free panko bread crumbs

Sweeteners:

Raw honey
Pure maple syrup
Coconut sugar
Stevia extract

Fruit:

Green apples
Bananas
Unsweetened, shredded coconut

Lemons
Frozen cherries
Frozen mango

Vegetables:

Cucumbers
Zucchini
Roasted red peppers
Onions
Romaine lettuce
Cucumbers
Zucchini
Roasted red peppers
Onions
Frozen green beans
Frozen butternut squash

Dry Goods:

Gluten-free pasta
White rice
Tortillas
Gluten-free bread
Sprouted pumpkin seeds

Soups:

Chicken broth
Beef broth

Oils/Fats:

Coconut oil
Olive oil
Avocado oil
Butter
Ghee

Spices:

Himalayan salt

White Pepper

Garlic powder (McCormick)

Ground coriander

Onion powder

Dill

Parsley

Basil

Thyme

Rosemary

Trader Joe's Everything Bagel spice blend (this does contain some high-oxalate spices: sea salt, garlic, onion, sesame seeds, black sesame seeds, and poppy seeds; use sparingly)

The Spice Hunter Mexican seasoning blend (this contains medium-high oxalate spices: cumin, onion, garlic, paprika, cilantro, red pepper, coriander, and oregano)

The Spice Hunter Herbes de Provence

Taco seasoning mix (chili powder, paprika, garlic powder, onion powder, oregano, crushed red pepper flakes, pepper, and salt)

Almond extract

Vanilla extract

Nutmeg

Cardamom

Condiments:

Dijon mustard

Avocado mayonnaise

Low-sugar ketchup

BBQ sauce

Salsa

Dairy:

Cheddar cheese

Feta cheese

Eggs

Sour cream

PART TWO

The Recipes

It can be confusing and overwhelming when you are first watching your oxalates. You're not only learning about them but trying to be diligent about consuming no- or low-oxalate foods and it can be so hard. I found it to be a real challenge.

When I began examining my diet I was blown away by how many foods contained high oxalates, almost all of my favorites. Adding to that, I needed to cook for my family. How was I supposed to make a meal for someone watching oxalates as well as those who can eat everything? Then on top of that everything needed to be gluten-free!

I'll often make side dishes for my family like French fries, baked potatoes, and pasta, and I'll double up on my low-ox veggies. It's second nature to me now and it will become easier for you too.

As I mentioned, I kept a list on my phone to refer to when I went grocery shopping which helped me and eventually I had my no- and low-oxalate foods memorized. Gluten-free shopping is much easier than it used to be since there are whole sections of the grocery store dedicated to GF foods.

This cookbook was designed for you, whether you are helping to monitor someone else or monitoring your own intake. Either way, I hope you find this book helpful and the recipes easy, satisfying, and delicious.

Main Courses

Cheeseburger Burritos 27

Baked Meatballs 28

Pork Cutlets with Sautéed Onions 28

Meatloaf with BBQ Sauce 29

Mexican Beef Wrap 31

Beef with Mushrooms 32

Low-Ox Vegetable Stir-Fry 33

Vegetarian Lasagna Bake 35

Crock-Pot Chicken 36

Meatloaf Sandwiches 38

Crispy Buttermilk Chicken 39

Beef and Noodles 40

Chicken Casserole with Rice 41

Chicken with Bacon 42

Chicken with Greek Seasoning 43

Hard Cider Braised Kielbasa 45

Stuffed Yellow (or Red) Peppers 46

Shrimp Jambalaya 48

Shrimp with Garlic and Lemon 50

Rice (or Quinoa) With Shrimp 51

Salmon Burger with Garlic Dill Aioli 53

Crispy Polenta 55

Cheeseburger Burritos

3-4 servings

My family can eat whatever they want; I'm the one with who is sensitive to gluten, sugar, oxalates, nuts, soy, yeast, and more. It can be challenging to come up with meals every night that will satisfy everyone. Here's an idea!

This meal can be modified depending on everyone's preferences and can be put together like a taco bar with ingredients set out for the family to pick and choose.

Get out these tools: knives, cutting board, skillet, cookie sheet, aluminum foil

1 lb. beef
2 tbsp olive oil
salt, pepper, garlic powder, to taste
1 white onion, chopped
tortillas (I use the gluten-free Udi's brand tortillas, slightly warmed)
8 slices of bacon, crispy
2 cups of cheddar cheese

1 tomato, sliced
1 avocado, cut into pieces
*Pan of cooked French fries (I like the gluten-free organic fries, they may be high depending on variety so use caution)
2 tbsp of each: ketchup (organic, low sugar), relish, mayonnaise (I like Vegenaise)

Brown beef in olive oil until cooked, and add salt, pepper, and garlic powder to flavor to suit your tastes. In a separate skillet, cook onion until it is translucent.

Lay a tortilla out on a plate and fill center with beef, add bacon, a little cheese, tomato, avocado, cooked onions, and French fries (yes, inside the burrito!). Add the ketchup, relish, mayo concoction, and fold it up, then cut in half.

NOTES

What I love about recipes like this is that the burritos are very easy to make and you can do the whole meal in thirty minutes.

The beef, bacon, onion, and avocado are all low-oxalate.

Depending on how strict you are with your oxalates, you can skip the French fries* and tortillas altogether and make a big salad from the ingredients listed. Ketchup does contain sugar, so be sure to look for a low-sugar version. I limit my tomatoes to a small slice.

*French fries are one of my treat foods that I eat sparingly; they fall between high- to very high-oxalate.

Baked Meatballs

4 servings

These meatballs are straightforward to make: nothing fancy or difficult. They pair well with pasta or rice, or between slices of bread for a meatball sandwich. Meat is free of oxalates, and I always make sure to get high-quality, organic, grass-fed beef.

Get out these tools: knives, cutting board, bowl, shallow pan or cookie sheet

1 lb. ground beef
1 egg
½ cup Parmesan cheese
½ cup gluten-free bread crumbs (may not be low, depends on the bread used, you can substitute Rice Chex, which is low)

1 tbsp minced garlic
1 tsp salt
1 tsp pepper (white pepper is lower in oxalates than black pepper)

Preheat oven to 400°F. Mix all ingredients in a large bowl and form into balls. Place in shallow pan and bake at 400°F for 20 minutes or until cooked through.

Pork Cutlets with Sautéed Onions

3-4 servings

When I'm tired of chicken and beef, I turn to pork. I buy cutlets, which are small and cook quickly. I probably cook these only a few times a year and when I do, I find that a simple seasoning with a thin crust works well. Pork pairs nicely with apples so if you like those flavors together, look at my recipe for Easy Applesauce (page 161).

Get out these tools: shallow dish or plate, skillet or pan, knives, cutting board

1 cup coconut flour
½ tsp garlic powder
½ tsp onion powder
4 boneless pork loin cutlets

1 tbsp olive oil
1 yellow onion, sliced
½ tsp salt

Mix coconut flour and spices in a shallow dish or plate. Dip each cutlet into flour mixture and cover both sides. Heat oil in pan and add cutlets, cooking on both sides over medium-high heat until cooked through, about three minutes on each side. Cutlets should be lightly browned on the outside.

Remove cutlets and add another tablespoon of olive oil to pan. Add sliced onion. Over high heat, sauté onion until it is soft and translucent. Serve on top of each pork cutlet. Season with more garlic powder and salt for your taste.

NOTE

Add more oil or butter to the sautéed onions if they are looking a little dry.

Meatloaf with BBQ Sauce

makes 1 meatloaf, serves 3-4

To me, meatloaf is total comfort food. Mashed potatoes, biscuits, meatloaf—somehow it all works together and seems ideal on a cold night. This meatloaf is made with BBQ sauce. I buy a gluten-free one that's low in sugar from Trader Joe's. The smoky flavor pairs well with beef. Ketchup-based sauces are lower in oxalates than tomato-paste-based sauce.

Get out these tools: knives, cutting board, bowl, cookie sheet, aluminum foil

1 lb. grass-fed, organic beef
2 eggs
½ cup gluten-free bread crumbs (make your own using Rice or Corn Chex)
½ cup gluten-free flour (Bob's Red Mill Coconut flour is low ox and so is Bob's Potato starch. I used Bob's gluten-free, but it hasn't been tested)
1 tsp garlic powder
¼ cup chopped onion
1 tbsp low-sugar ketchup
1 tbsp BBQ★ sauce (I get the ★gluten-free sauce from Trader Joe's) plus an additional tbsp for top of meatloaf.

Mix all ingredients by hand in a large bowl. Arrange on lined cookie sheet in a loaf form. Top with 1 tablespoon of BBQ sauce.

Bake for 1 hour at 350°F.

NOTE

Ketchup-based BBQ sauces are lower in oxalates than tomato-sauce-based, but as far as I have seen, it has not been tested for oxalates. Here's a super quick and easy recipe for a ketchup-based sauce:

1½ cup ketchup

¼ cup mustard

¼ cup honey or brown sugar (I use coconut sugar)

Use an immersion blender to mix well.

Mexican Beef Wrap

1-2 servings

Wraps can be made to suit everyone's individual preferences and are easy to throw together for lunch or dinner. You can turn this into a salad by skipping the wrap and using low-oxalate lettuce like romaine or iceberg. Ground beef, cilantro, avocado, and cheese are all low in oxalates.

Get out these tools: knives, cutting board, skillet, bowl for mixing dressing

⅓ cup ground beef
½ onion
1–3 teaspoons Spice Hunter Mexican Blend (or more, to taste)
gluten-free wrap, such as Udi's plain tortilla
2 tbsp cotija cheese
½ cup chopped cilantro
½ avocado

Brown the beef in a skillet. Add onion and sauté until onion is soft. Add the Spice Hunter's Mexican Blend. Start with 1 teaspoon and increase until it's to your desired spice level. If you don't have this blend, you can use ½ cumin (½ tsp is medium ox) and ½ teaspoon garlic, adjusting to suit your taste. You can use a splash of Tabasco for heat.

After the beef is cooked, lay out the wrap and add the beef, cheese, cilantro, and avocado. Top with dressing and roll up.

Dressing:
¼ cup olive oil
¼ salsa (picante sauce—may vary; Tabasco sauce is low)
½ cup sour cream

Mix all ingredients together, blending well.

NOTE

If you don't have a gluten-free wrap, you can serve beef over tortilla chips or rice (cauliflower rice) or a combination of the two. If you don't have cotija cheese, cheddar works fine. Cotija has a bit of saltiness to it, eliminating the need for salt.

Beef with Mushrooms

3-4 servings

Mushrooms are a very low-oxalate vegetable with several health benefits. While I'm pretty unlikely to grab a handful of mushrooms for a snack, I'm open to using them in a dish like this one. Beef and mushrooms are such a classic combination.

Mushrooms are not only low in calories, but they are cholesterol-free and low in sodium. They contain B vitamins, selenium, niacin, copper, and potassium.

Get out these tools: knives, cutting board, two skillets

3 tbsp bacon grease or butter
1 small onion, chopped
1 cup of mushrooms, cleaned and cut into
    pieces, stems removed (I used white button
    mushrooms)
1 lb. ground beef
1 egg

1 tsp onion powder
1 tsp garlic powder
¼ cup coconut flour
2 cups beef broth
1 tsp coconut aminos
¾ cup sour cream
salt and white pepper

In a small skillet heat 1 tablespoon of bacon grease/butter until melted then add chopped onion and mushrooms. Set on medium heat and stir occasionally until mushrooms are browned and onion is soft.

In a large skillet, melt remaining bacon grease/butter. While it melts, mix beef, egg, onion and garlic powders, and coconut flour in a bowl and shape into patties. Add mix to skillet.

Heat for a few minutes on each side, and then add broth and coconut aminos. Place lid over pan and let beef cook, turning over every four minutes until patties are cooked through.

Transfer meat to a plate and, with heat on medium-low, add sour cream to broth, and stir until sour cream and broth are blended. Add meat to pan along with mushrooms and onions. Sprinkle with additional garlic powder, salt, and pepper as needed.

NOTE

A side of gluten-free pasta or rice goes well with this dish; cauliflower rice is also a great side, plus some homemade applesauce. It's a nice, warm comfort food meal.

Low-Ox Vegetable Stir-Fry

4-5 servings

This is one of those last-minute meals where you wonder how you're going to pull off dinner with only thirty minutes until everyone gets hungry and grumpy.

What do you have in the fridge? Pull it all out. Chop it up. Throw it in the skillet with some olive or avocado oil. Shake in some spices. Do you have a rotisserie chicken in the fridge? Pull off some pieces and add to the stir-fry, heating it all together.

Serve it over rice, pasta, or cauliflower rice. Set out the coconut aminos in place of soy sauce. You don't even have to bother measuring, just pull it out, chop it up, and heat thoroughly.

Get out these tools: knives, cutting board, skillet

1 head of cauliflower
2 bok choy
1 red pepper
1 zucchini
1 small onion
bunch of mushrooms
1 head of cabbage
1–2 tbsp of olive oil, ghee, or avocado oil
garlic powder (start with 1 tsp)
salt and white pepper
coconut aminos

In a large skillet, add all the vegetables, turn heat to medium, and sauté in oil. This should take about ten to fifteen minutes; frequently stir the veggies around so everything cooks evenly. The zucchini will probably start to soften first. Add in your garlic powder, salt, and pepper. Remember the white pepper is potent!

If you have a rotisserie chicken on hand, add some pieces toward the end of the stir-frying of the vegetables so it heats up a little.

Shake in a little of the coconut aminos if you want, or let everyone add their own, which is my preference. I like it, but my husband prefers regular soy sauce, so I also have that on hand for him.

Serve it up on a bowl, over white rice or gluten-free pasta if you want. A nice big bowl of low-oxalate fruit would go well with this!

Vegetarian Lasagna Bake

3-4 servings

I have a new appreciation for zucchini. It's a superstar that can be baked, sautéed, made into noodles (see zoodles), and is low in oxalates. It contains anti-inflammatory properties and is low in carbs and calories. This green veg is high in folate, vitamin K, potassium, and riboflavin.

Similar to zucchini is yellow squash. It too can be eaten raw and made into a variety of dishes. Yellow squash contains vitamin B6, folate, magnesium, potassium, and manganese, just to name a few nutrients.

This "lasagna" combines these two low-oxalate powerhouses and pairs well with the meatball recipe or stands on its own!

Get out these tools: knives, cutting board, bowl, 8 x 8-inch pan

2 medium zucchini, washed and sliced thin
2 yellow squash, washed and sliced thin
1 tsp olive oil
½ tsp garlic powder
½ tsp onion powder

salt and white pepper
3 cups of homemade tomato sauce (oxalate levels
    may vary, medium to high)
1 cup of mozzarella cheese
1 tsp basil (medium oxalate)

Preheat oven to 375°F.

Toss zucchini and squash with olive oil, garlic and onion powders, salt and pepper.

In 8 x 8-inch pan, coat bottom with sauce. Layer squash and zucchini, then sauce, then mozzarella cheese, and repeat. Sprinkle with fresh basil and cover with foil.

Bake at 375°F for 45 minutes, until vegetables are soft.

NOTES

A can of conventional tomato sauce is high in oxalates, so I prefer to make my own using fresh tomatoes which might keep the content of oxalates down a little. I limit my consumption of tomatoes, but I do love them and enjoy them on occasion.

Try this with Roasted Red Pepper sauce to keep oxalates low.

Crock-Pot Chicken

4 servings

When time is short and you need something for dinner, there's nothing like busting out the Crock-Pot. Set it on low, throw in some ingredients, and, within a few hours, it's going to be hot and ready!

I serve this over rice noodles (or rice) with a side of bok choy.

Get out these tools: Crock-Pot, knives, cutting board

10 frozen chicken tenders (instead of large chicken breasts, I like the smaller tenders)
1 tsp minced garlic
2 cups chicken broth
2 tbsp fresh basil, cut into small pieces
1 tsp salt
¼ cup cilantro
¼ cup olive oil
1 tbsp coconut aminos
salt, as needed
squeeze of juice from ½ lime
8 ounces water chestnuts

Place tenders in Crock-Pot along with everything but water chestnuts. Cook on low for 2 to 3 hours or until chicken is tender and no longer pink inside. Cut chicken into chunks and add water chestnuts. Serve in bowls over rice noodles.

NOTE

I like rice noodles, but you can use zoodles too. This recipe will have a lot of liquid left over, which is why I like to serve it in bowls.

Meatloaf Sandwiches

1–2 servings

Cook one meatloaf and get two meals out of it! The leftover meatloaf and onion rings are piled onto this sandwich for a quick meal. I love leftovers, and I'm always sad when I don't have them.

Get out these tools: knives, cutting board, cookie sheet

1 tsp olive oil
gluten-free buns (might be medium to high-ox, check ingredients)
1 tsp garlic powder
leftover meatloaf (page 29), sliced
leftover onion rings (page 139)
4 slices of crisp bacon
1 tbsp BBQ sauce

Lightly drizzle olive oil over inside of buns and sprinkle with garlic powder. Lightly toast. Reheat meatloaf slices and onion rings.

Pile meatloaf, onion rings, and bacon on toasted buns and top with BBQ sauce.

NOTES

There's something that works really well with the BBQ and bacon flavors along with the onion rings. I'm getting hungry just thinking about it.

If you need a bun to make this sandwich come alive, I like the gluten-free buns from Trader Joe's or Canyon Bakehouse, though, to my knowledge, they have not been tested for oxalates.

Always read the ingredients on store-bought baked goods to double-check their oxalate count; even gluten-free items can contain high-oxalate ingredients. This was something I had to learn. At first I had assumed that everything gluten-free is also low-oxalate, but that's not so! It all depends on which flour is used, how much is used, and how many servings you have.

Crispy Buttermilk Chicken

3-4 servings

When you are gluten-free, you miss certain things. And not that I'd often have crispy chicken, but it would be really nice to eat it if I wanted it. And if I want it, I'm going to have to make it myself, because I have only found one place to get gluten-free crispy chicken and it's in Vancouver, nowhere near where I live!

Here's a recipe that is made with gluten-free ingredients and is cooked in avocado oil, which has a higher smoke point than olive oil so the oil gets hot, but doesn't burn.

Get out these tools: ziplock plastic baggie, large bowl, skillet**,** knives, cookie sheet, and parchment paper

8 chicken tenders
1 cup gluten-free flour
1 cup *GF panko bread crumbs (I do not have oxalate count of Panko, see below note)
1 tsp. garlic powder
1 tsp onion powder
1 tsp paprika
1 tsp baking powder

¾ tsp baking soda
¼ cup avocado oil
2 tbsp butter

Marinade
1 cup buttermilk
1 tsp paprika (paprika is medium ox per 1 tsp)
1 tsp garlic powder

Marinate the chicken in plastic bag for 2 to 3 hours with the buttermilk, paprika, and garlic powder.

After chicken has marinated, combine flour, panko, spices, baking powder and soda, and flour in a medium bowl.

Heat ¼ cup avocado oil plus 2 tablespoons butter in a skillet. Dip chicken in flour mixture coating well, drop into hot oil/butter in skillet. Cook for about four minutes each side or until golden brown.

Put chicken on a parchment-lined cookie sheet. Finish baking in oven for 15 to 20 minutes or until no longer pink inside.

NOTE

Make your own low-oxalate panko bread crumbs by using about six cups of Rice Chex, which will make two cups of crumbs. Simply pulverize the Chex in your food processor, then add salt and white pepper. I will often make several cups to keep on hand and store in the pantry.

Beef and Noodles

4 servings

This is a quick and simplified take on beef Stroganoff. I always keep beef and chicken broth in the pantry along with sour cream in the fridge. When you have the staples, you can throw a meal together quickly even at the last minute. Keeping your pantry and fridge stocked with low-oxalate options is a lifesaver.

Get out these tools: knives, cutting board, skillet

1 tbsp butter
1 cup of white mushrooms, cleaned and cut into pieces
garlic clove, chopped into pieces or 1 tablespoon minced garlic
1 small onion
1 lb. beef, browned and set aside
2 cups beef broth
½ cup sour cream
gluten-free pasta, cooked according to directions (I like the gluten-free brown rice pasta from Tinkyada)
salt and pepper, to taste
1–2 tbsp fresh parsley, minced

In a skillet over medium-high heat, melt butter and add mushrooms, garlic, and onion, sauté until soft. Add the browned beef and combine. Pour in broth and sour cream. Mix gently. Add cooked gluten-free noodles, turn heat to low, and mix everything together. Add salt, pepper, and parsley as desired.

Chicken Casserole with Rice

4-5 servings

It was one of those nights when I didn't know what I was going to make for dinner and the clock was inching toward 5 p.m. Looking in the pantry, I saw rice, and the chicken was already defrosted. I came up with this at the last minute and thank goodness everyone liked it. This casserole reminds me of a cold night in New Jersey where I grew up. There is something soothing about a hot casserole (or soup) on a chilly evening.

Get out these tools: soup pot, skillet, cutting board, bowl, large casserole dish

4 tbsp butter, divided
6–8 chicken tenders or 4 chicken breasts
1 cup broth
1 onion
2–3 cups of white rice, cooked per directions on bag
1 tsp garlic powder

1 cup of mayonnaise mixed with ¾ cup sour cream (use this instead of canned cream soup)
2 cups cheddar cheese
2 cups boiled ★broccoli, drained and cut into pieces
salt and white pepper

Melt 3 tablespoons butter in a skillet, and add chicken and broth. Cook chicken in a deep skillet on stovetop. If you are working with frozen chicken, simmer in broth for about twenty minutes or until it's cooked through, checking frequently and turning over so it cooks evenly. Remove chicken and cut into pieces, then set aside.

Add remaining 1 tablespoon butter to pan and sauté onion until soft.

Mix cooked rice, onion, chicken, garlic powder, plus mayo and sour cream in a medium bowl.

To that mixture, add the cheddar cheese, broccoli, salt, and white pepper then spread into a medium casserole dish.

Pop in 350°F oven for 10 to 15 minutes until cheese is melted.

NOTE

Broccoli is considered medium oxalate, but ½ cup of boiled broccoli is low-oxalate.

Chicken with Bacon

4 servings

I'm sure you know that chicken is a lean meat and fantastic source of protein. It contains phosphorus and calcium, plus two nutrients that are linked to helping with stress, tryptophan and vitamin B5.

Chicken is also low in fat and is a good source of healthy omega-3 fatty acids.

A ½ cup serving of tomato paste is high in oxalates, so I use the minimal amount in this dish. The low-oxalate coconut flour and oil work nicely with the chicken, and the flavor of bacon gives the chicken dish a punch of flavor. This pairs well with rice or served over pasta (or zoodles) alongside steamed vegetables for a hearty, filling meal.

To cook the bacon quickly and easily, line a cookie sheet with foil and spread out the bacon strips. Place in the oven and turn to 425°F. While the oven heats, the bacon cooks!

When the bacon is crispy, remove from oven and pour leftover bacon grease into a glass dish, then use to cook the chicken for this recipe. Rest the bacon on paper towels and blot excess grease.

Get out these tools: cookie sheet, ziplock baggie, aluminum foil, bowl, knives, cutting board, skillet, pan, whisk

8–10 bacon strips
1 cup coconut flour
1 tsp onion powder
salt and white pepper, adjusted to your taste
8 chicken tenders or 4 breasts, cut into strips
⅓ cup coconut oil (or bacon grease)

2 cups of chicken broth
2 tbsp tomato paste (1 tbsp of Hunts tomato paste is low-ox, 2 tbsp is medium-ox)
½ cup dry red wine
1 tsp thyme
1 tsp chopped garlic

Put the bacon in the oven so it can crisp up and be ready when you need it.

Combine coconut flour, onion powder, salt, and pepper in a 1-gallon ziplock bag and give it a good shake. Add the chicken tenders and shake it up to coat each piece.

Melt coconut oil/bacon grease in a skillet set to medium heat. Drop chicken pieces one by one and brown, flipping over every three minutes until cooked through.

Remove chicken to plate and pour broth, tomato paste, and wine into pan, using a whisk to combine. Add salt, white pepper, thyme, and garlic; allow it to simmer. After ten minutes, reduce heat and add chicken, making sure to coat each piece.

Crumble bacon and sprinkle over chicken.

> **NOTE**
> The alcohol in the wine cooks off but flavor remains. I buy bacon that is no-nitrate and organic. If you cannot tolerate bacon due to histamines, leave it off; the chicken will still taste delicious!

Chicken with Greek Seasoning

3-4 servings

I love Greek flavors! I like to use basil, thyme, fennel, rosemary, mint, garlic, onion, dill, and bay leaves in my dishes to get that delicious Greek flavor. Just remember to take out the bay leaf!

Get out these tools: ziplock baggie, knives, cutting board, shallow dish

6–8 chicken tenders
½ cup olive oil
1-2 tbsp fresh dill
1-2 tbsp thyme

1 tsp onion powder
1 tsp garlic powder
salt and pepper

Place chicken tenders, olive oil, and spices in a large ziplock bag and allow to marinate for 2 to 3 hours or longer.

When you're ready to cook the chicken, pour into shallow dish and bake covered with foil, at 450°F for 15 to 20 minutes. Uncover and allow chicken to sit for ten minutes.

NOTE

This goes nicely with the Tzatziki Sauce. The chicken can be cooked then cooled and cut into pieces for a salad. I love a good leftover, and this chicken makes a nice addition to salad along with some feta cheese.

Hard Cider Braised Kielbasa

4 servings

Kielbasa is a smoked sausage coming to us from Poland. Thank you, Poland, I love it! Originally it was made with pork, but now you can buy it made from beef or turkey. With a garlicky, smoky flavor, kielbasa doesn't need any additional spices.

I always buy the no-nitrate, organic, gluten-free kielbasa.

Get out these tools: knives, cutting board, pan or deep skillet

2 tbsp butter or coconut oil, melted
¼ yellow onion, chopped
1 package of no-nitrate organic kielbasa (I buy it from Sprouts)
½ cup hard apple cider (I buy it from Trader Joe's)

Melt butter or oil in large pan; add onion and sauté until onion is soft.

Slice kielbasa into bite-size pieces and add to pan with onions. Heat kielbasa. Pour in cider and simmer on medium heat until cider has thickened and kielbasa is heated through.

NOTE

I like this with rice or cauliflower rice with a side of zucchini. You really can't go wrong with this simple main course.

Stuffed Yellow (or Red) Peppers

2 servings

I was sad to learn that green bell peppers were medium in oxalates, I loved green pepper in an omelet. But happy news! Yellow, orange, and red peppers are lower in oxalates than green.

Yellow peppers are medium; you can use red or orange if medium ox isn't an issue. Both are lower than yellow, which is at the upper end of the medium range.

Yellow peppers contain vitamins C and B6, plus folate, potassium, and copper. These peppers help to decrease risk for heart disease, high cholesterol, and cancer. Yellow peppers boost the immune system and help remove the free radicals that cause cancer and inflammation. If you cannot tolerate yellow, you can use red peppers here.

Get out these tools: knives, cutting board, skillet, cookie sheet or shallow dish

2 cups of cauliflower rice or regular rice
½ tsp ground red pepper, or less
salt as needed
1 cup cleaned, cooked shrimp (I buy cleaned, precooked, frozen shrimp and let it defrost)
squeeze of lime juice (from half of a lime)
2 large yellow or red peppers, halved and seeds removed
1 cup cheddar cheese
1 avocado, sliced
⅓ cup cilantro, chopped
2 tbsp salsa or picante sauce (levels vary, see if you can tolerate 2 tbsp)

Heat oven to 375°F. While oven preheats, heat cauliflower rice in skillet, add spices and shrimp over medium heat, mixing through. Squeeze lime juice over mixture.

Stuff half of rice/shrimp in each pepper and top with cheddar cheese. Bake for twenty minutes or until cheese is melted. Remove from heat and add avocado, cilantro, and salsa.

Shrimp Jambalaya

3-4 servings

This dish is so easy to prepare. Basically, you are just combining the ingredients. I love a quick, easy, low-oxalate dinner that's ready in less than thirty minutes. And if the cleanup is quick, then it's a meal I will definitely make again.

Get out these tools: skillet, knives, cutting board

1 white onion, diced
1 tbsp garlic
1 tbsp olive oil
1 yellow bell pepper, diced (use red if oxalates in yellow are too high)
1 lb. precooked frozen shrimp, defrosted
1 kielbasa, cut into pieces
1 can crushed tomatoes, if tolerated—can be high-oxalate
½ tsp red pepper
2 cups cooked rice/cauliflower rice
salt + white pepper

Sauté onion and garlic in a skillet with olive oil. Add pepper. Add shrimp and kielbasa, and cook thoroughly. Toss in the crushed tomatoes and red pepper. The last step is adding in the rice and mixing it all up. Add the salt and white pepper as needed.

NOTE

To add more heat and spice, I'd usually add cumin, but it's very high in oxalates. Low-oxalate heat can come from crushed red pepper flakes, dried cayenne pepper, or Tabasco.

Shrimp with Garlic and Lemon

4 servings

Shrimp is low in calories and high in niacin and selenium as well as the antioxidant astaxanthin. Try to buy shrimp that is wild, not farm raised, since farm-raised shrimp may contain illegal chemicals and antibiotics. Shrimp is delicious cooked in butter with garlic. It's a classic pairing!

Get out these tools: knives, cutting board, pan or deep skillet

2 tbsp butter
2 cloves of garlic, chopped
1 lb. shrimp (pre-cleaned and precooked, available in the frozen section of store)
1 tsp basil
1 tsp rosemary
1 tsp thyme
1 tbsp fresh lemon juice
salt + white pepper

Melt butter in pan. Sauté garlic then add shrimp, cooking on medium heat until shrimp is browned. In a small bowl, mix spices then add to shrimp. Add the lemon juice, salt, and pepper, adjusting to suit your taste. Add more spices by the ½ teaspoon until you get the flavor you desire.

This is such an easy and quick main dish. I can't believe I used to be afraid of cooking shrimp! I guess still am, which is why I buy the precooked frozen kind.

Rice (or Quinoa) with Shrimp

3-4 servings

If you are highly sensitive to oxalates, swap out the quinoa in this recipe for cauliflower rice or white rice. I have found some conflicting information regarding quinoa (some says high in oxalates, other information indicates it's medium), so if you have leaky gut, I'd skip the quinoa in favor of cauliflower rice.

I am including it here for those who may not be watching their oxalates as closely as others. Quinoa is high in protein, fiber, and magnesium. I wish I could consume it, but it's on the "too high for me" list. My family can eat it, though, so I will make it for them and heat up my little cup of cauliflower rice.

Get out these tools: knives, cutting board, bowl

Quinoa and Shrimp:

1 cup quinoa★ (or white rice) cooked
1 cup cooked shrimp
½ cucumber, chopped
½ yellow pepper, chopped (use red for lower oxalates)
¼ cup feta cheese
½ tomato, sliced
2 cups romaine or iceberg lettuce

Assemble all ingredients in large bowl, and toss with Red Wine Vinaigrette.

Red Wine Vinaigrette:

½ cup olive oil
¼ cup red wine vinegar
1 tbsp chopped fresh oregano, if tolerated
salt and white pepper

Mix ingredients in a bowl and drizzle over shrimp salad.

NOTE

Add crisp bacon bits, gluten-free croutons, avocado, red pepper to make this a super filling salad.

*Since quinoa is extremely high, you might want to use millet; when soaked millet is medium per cup and even if not soaked, it's lower than quinoa. I use cauliflower rice.

Salmon Burger with Garlic Dill Aioli

makes enough for 2–3 burgers

You could go through the hassle of cooking your own salmon burgers, but I like to buy them already made to save time. I get these at Trader Joe's and they cook up quickly with no mess.

Get out these tools: knives, cutting board, spoons, mixing bowl

salmon burger (I use the Premium Salmon Burgers from Trader Joe's)
¼ cup avocado mayo
1 tbsp minced garlic
½ tsp salt
½ tsp white pepper or less
1 tbsp fresh dill, chopped

Cook salmon burger according to instructions on package. Mix all aioli ingredients in a small bowl, taste, and season to suit your preferences. I always like a heavier hand with the salt and garlic.

NOTE

I skip bread completely and wrap the burger in a large romaine lettuce leaf. This would taste so good on a lightly toasted bun (gluten-free of course, and always check ingredients).

Crispy Polenta

2-3 servings

I used to see polenta at the store and think, "What do you do with that?" and I'd keep on walking down the aisle. Then I had some delicious polenta on a cruise and started buying it to make at home. Cooked up nice and crispy, it makes a tasty side dish or even a main course.

Get out these tools: knives, cutting board, skillet

prepared polenta (I use Ancient Grains Polenta)
1 tbsp olive oil
1 tbsp butter

Slice polenta into ½-inch-thick pieces. Add olive oil and butter into skillet, set heat to medium-high.

Add polenta rounds to hot skillet and cook 5 to 8 minutes on each side, until it's equally crispy. Polenta should be nicely brown and crisp.

Lay polenta on paper towels to blot excess grease. Salt and pepper as needed.

NOTE

If you've never tried polenta, I encourage you to give it a whirl! It's a nice alternative to rice or pasta. Warning: your stovetop will need a good cleaning after frying these up!

I like Ancient Grains Gluten-Free Polenta, which is Non-GMO Project verified. The ingredients are: water, organic yellow cornmeal, salt, tartaric acid, ascorbic acid, and beta-carotene.

Soups and Salads

Greek Salad with Fresh Herbs

1-2 servings

I make this salad almost every day for lunch. Add whatever low-oxalate foods you want to create a filling meal. To save time and dishes, I buy a rotisserie chicken and cut off pieces for my daily salads.

Get out these tools: knives, cutting board, salad spinner, small bowl

Salad:

2 cups of chopped romaine or iceberg lettuce
½ cucumber, chopped
¼ cup feta cheese
¼ cup roasted red peppers
kalamata olives★ (these are high-oxalate, so I
    only eat two or three)

¼ cup red onion
¼ cup fresh tomato, if tolerated
1 tbsp fresh dill
1 tbsp thyme

Mix all ingredients together and drizzle with dressing.

Dressing:

½ cup olive oil
juice of small lemon

salt, white pepper
2 tbsp red wine vinegar

Whisk ingredients together in a small bowl.

NOTES

Though kalamata and black olives may be high-oxalate, in moderation they don't bother me; however, I eat very few and consume them sparingly. I add them to my Greek salad once in a while.

If you are closely monitoring your oxalate levels, you can skip them.

For 10 black olives:

Total Oxalate Value: 12.90 mg

Soluble Oxalates: 4.63 mg

10 green olives:

Total Oxalate Value: 27.42 mg

Soluble Oxalates: 0.72 mg

2 tablespoons of capers, which offer the salty flavor of olives could be an alternative:

Total Oxalate Value: 1.59 mg

Soluble Oxalates: 0.93 mg

Salade Niçoise

1-2 servings

The traditional Salade Niçoise comes to us from Nice, France, and was initially made with tomatoes, anchovies, artichokes, plus olive oil, red peppers, black olives. It did not contain tuna or lettuce, which is a staple of the modern Salade Niçoise.

Wouldn't it be amazing to have a traditional Salade Niçoise while in Nice, France? I'll just have to settle for my kitchen table in southern California.

Get out these tools: knives, cutting board, salad spinner, bowl to mix dressing

Salad:

2 cups iceberg or romaine lettuce
3 pieces of crisp bacon, crumbled
2 hard-boiled eggs, halved
½ cup tuna

⅓ cup green beans★, cooked and cut into pieces
¼ cup tomatoes, optional
1 teaspoon capers, optional

Assemble all ingredients on a plate and drizzle with Dijon dressing.

Dressing:

¼ cup olive oil
1 tsp basil
1 tsp thyme
½ tsp garlic powder

1 tsp salt
1 tsp Dijon mustard
½ tsp fresh lemon juice

Whisk all ingredients together until completely blended.

NOTE

I boil the green beans and throw out the water to decrease oxalates. Oxalates in beans will vary based on variety; cut Roma beans are medium to low oxalate.

Green Beans

Total Oxalate Value: 24.36 mg

Soluble Oxalates: 12.22 mg

Tuna Salad on Lettuce

1–2 servings

When I get in a rut with my daily salads, I turn to tuna. High in protein, tuna is filling and pairs well with the dill and a splash of lemon juice. Instead of eating it on bread, I use lettuce, like a lettuce wrap.

Get out these tools: salad spinner, knives, cutting board, bowl for mixing

1 can tuna, drained
½ cup Vegenaise or avocado oil mayo
¼ cup chopped cucumber
1 tsp. dill
½ tsp salt
squeeze of fresh lemon
romaine lettuce leaves

Mix all ingredients except romaine. Scoop tuna salad onto individual leaves and serve immediately.

Soups and Salads

Creamy Zucchini Soup

3-4 servings

I had some extra zucchini that I didn't know what to do with, so I decided to create a soup. I used my leftover half-and-half which I had in the fridge from the Butternut Squash Soup.

This needed a little something else, so I topped it with Parmesan cheese. I absolutely love soups like this one. You can easily modify to satisfy your preferences, putting in more or less spices, add different cheese . . . feel free to experiment.

Get out these tools: large soup pot, knives, cutting board, immersion blender

3 medium zucchini cut into chunks
1 small yellow onion
1 tbsp minced garlic
2 tbsp of butter
5 cups chicken broth
½ cup half-and-half
Parmesan cheese
1 tbsp basil
1 tsp of Herbs de Provence★ spice
1 tsp onion powder
salt and pepper

Sauté zucchini, onion, garlic, and butter in soup pot until zucchini is soft and onion is translucent.

Add chicken broth and bring to a boil. Remove from heat, add the measured herbs (or more, to taste), and blend with immersion blender, add half-and-half, and return to a low heat.

Top with a sprinkle of Parmesan cheese and additional salt and pepper as needed.

NOTE

Herbs de Provence have not been tested and contain varied ingredients. The Herbs de Provence mixture I use from the Spice Hunter contains thyme, rosemary, basil, majoram, sage, fennel, and lavender.

Butternut Squash Soup

3-4 servings

I really like a hot, hearty soup. Years ago I would have turned away from butternut squash, but I have really grown to like it. It is especially good in this soup, which is perfect on a cold night.

Butternut squash contains vitamin A, potassium, calcium, and fiber. It's also high in antioxidants.

Get out these tools: large soup pot, knives, cutting board, immersion blender

2 tbsp of butter
1 small yellow onion, chopped
2 10-oz. bags of frozen organic butternut squash
1 tsp garlic powder
½ tsp onion powder
½ tsp sage
½ tsp basil
1 tsp salt, to taste
4 cups chicken broth
½ cup heavy cream or half-and-half

In large soup pot, melt butter and sauté onion until translucent and soft. Add butternut squash and spices, continue to sauté over medium-high heat.

Add four cups chicken broth to pot and bring to a boil, allow to simmer for ten minutes so spices and flavors can blend.

Remove from heat and, using an immersion blender, blend until smooth. Add ½ cup cream then return to low heat and stir until heated through.

(Chicken) Bone Broth

3-4 servings

The benefits of bone broth are numerous, especially for those who have leaky gut. The gelatin from the broth helps to seal up gaps or holes in the intestines (hence the leaky gut), plus the broth is an excellent source of collagen, and the various nutrients in the broth increase immune function.

I make bone broth and use it in place of chicken broth in recipes. The flavor of homemade bone broth is richer than anything store-bought.

Get out these tools: Crock-Pot, knives, cutting board, strainer

bones from 1 whole organic chicken
8 cups of water
1 small white onion, chopped
1 clove of garlic
2 carrots, chopped
1 handful of parsley, chopped
Himalayan sea salt (I grind it in generously)
1 tbsp of apple cider vinegar

Place all of the ingredients in a Crock-Pot/slow cooker. Cook on low heat for 24 hours. Halfway through, I break up the bones so the marrow can leak out.

When the broth is done cooking, place a strainer over a large pot and pour the soup over the strainer. What you're left with is a healthy broth that can be consumed any time of the day.

NOTES

Bone broth is high in histamines, so if you struggle with histamine levels, skip the bones in this recipe. Try boiling chicken breasts/boneless chicken parts instead to get the beneficial amino acids.

Bone broth isn't high-oxalate, but it's rich in glycine and other aminos. Because these can convert to oxalate, it should be used cautiously and in smaller servings

Cauliflower Soup with Bacon

3-4 servings

Cauliflower is a superstar vegetable. Thank goodness it's low in oxalates and can be cooked a wide variety of ways, making it one of my go-to ingredients.

It's also very good for you, containing the following: vitamin C, vitamin K, folate, pantothenic acid, vitamin B6 plus fiber, omega-3 fatty acids, manganese, phosphorus, and biotin! Cauliflower is also anti-inflammatory and, like other cruciferous vegetables, helps fight disease thanks to its many nutrients.

This soup in particular is really tasty with the bacon crumbles. Chives and cheddar cheese plus sour cream all work well too.

Get out these tools: large soup pot, knives, cutting board, immersion blender

2 tbsp butter
2 tbsp gluten-free flour
½ onion, diced
1 cauliflower, stem removed and chopped into pieces
½ tsp garlic powder
salt and pepper, to taste

32 oz. chicken broth (I use organic, low-sodium broth)
6 slices of bacon, crumbled, for garnish
1 tbsp sour cream, for garnish
¼ cup chives, for garnish
1 cup cheddar cheese, for garnish

In a large soup pot, melt better over medium flame and whisk in the flour. Add onion, cauliflower, spices, and broth.

Simmer until cauliflower is softened, about 25 minutes.

Remove from heat and use an immersion blender until smooth. Do a taste test and adjust the spices. I always like more salt and garlic powder, so I add ½ teaspoon of each until it tastes right. Feel free to add what you want to make this delicious for you. A little more pepper, a little less salt.

In each bowl, add crumbled bacon along with sour cream, chives, and cheese adjusted for each person's taste.

> **NOTES**
>
> Cauliflower is one of those low-oxalate vegetables that you can make many ways. You can roast it, mash it, eat it raw, and turn it into a soup like this one. The traditional cauliflower soup recipe calls for leeks, but they are medium to high in oxalates. If you can tolerate leeks, swap out the onion for them.
>
> **Leeks, ½ cup**
>
> Total Oxalate Value: 7.65 mg
>
> Soluble Oxalates: 4.23 mg

Tomato Soup

1–2 servings

I used to love going out to eat and ordering tomato soup especially at Nordstrom! They had the most delicious soup, and I often bought a jar to take home. When I started having food allergies I had to very carefully determine what soups contained gluten, high oxalates, too much sugar, soy, and yeast—it became difficult to eat at restaurants.

I discovered I could make my own soup from leftover tomato sauce and it satisfies my craving. Because of the oxalates in tomatoes, I eat them sparingly. Skip this recipe if you are strictly keeping to a low-oxalate diet.

Get out these tools: large soup pot, blender

1½ cups leftover tomato sauce
½ cup half-and-half
⅓ cup chicken broth
1 tsp garlic powder
salt and pepper

Add all ingredients to blender and combine. Pour into soup pot and stir over medium-high heat until it's hot and bubbling. If the soup is too thick, add more chicken broth until it's a consistency you like.

Garnish with fresh basil and Parmesan cheese (mozzarella works too).

NOTE

Based on the number of servings this might be too high for someone avoiding medium to high-oxalate foods.

Turkey Sausage and Vegetable Soup

3-4 servings

I like buying the sausage in bulk form, which is the meat and spices minus the sausage casing. This soup just screams "winter" to me. It's filled with veggies and you can always adjust the amount.

Sausage is high in vitamins D and B12, high in protein and selenium. I consume it sparingly, however, because it's also high in histamines and is a processed food. For some recipes, however, sausage adds just the right amount of flavor.

Get out these tools: pan/skillet, knives, cutting board, soup pot

1 tbsp olive oil
1 lb. turkey sausage
½ head of cauliflower, chopped
2–3 carrots (boiled to decrease oxalates), chopped
2 small zucchini, cut into pieces
1 yellow onion
1 tsp garlic powder
1 tsp onion powder
1 tsp parsley
32 oz. chicken broth
1 can diced tomatoes with juice (high to very high-oxalate)

Heat oil in large pan/skillet and add turkey sausage, cooking until no longer pink. Remove sausage and add cauliflower, carrots, zucchini, and onion. Heat until soft.

In soup pot, add sausage, spices, vegetables, broth, and tomatoes and cook on low heat for a half hour until flavors are combined. Taste and adjust spices. Serve with freshly grated Parmesan cheese sprinkled on top.

NOTES

I'd usually make this with potatoes, but to keep the oxalate level low, I used cauliflower. You can toss in any other low-ox vegetable you want to really give this soup more nutrients; some other low-oxalate options are butternut squash, mushrooms, and red peppers. Use ½ cup diced tomatoes if using the whole can is too many oxalates.

Canned Peeled Tomatoes, ½ cup

Total Oxalate Value: 15.24 mg

Soluble Oxalates: 3.72 mg

Herbed Chicken Soup

3-4 servings

Even if you are not a big fan of getting in the kitchen and cooking, I promise that soups are very easy to prepare. Do the prep work, throw it all in the Crock-Pot, and walk away for a few hours.

The flavors come together as the vegetables cook, and when it's finished, you really only have to do the garnishes and a side dish such as some popovers or muffins. Leftover soups are also great for lunch!

Get out these tools: Crock-Pot, cutting board, knives, pan or skillet to sauté, spiralizer

2 tbsp minced garlic
½ small onion, chopped
1 tbsp butter
2 cups cooked chicken, chopped into pieces
⅓ cup boiled carrots, chopped
1 tsp onion powder
1 tbsp Herbs de Province
32 oz. chicken broth (low-sodium, organic)
1 tsp coconut aminos (skip this if you aren't a fan of the flavor)
salt and white pepper, to taste

In a pan, sauté garlic and onion in butter until soft and fragrant. Place all other ingredients in a Crock-Pot, then add garlic and onions. Set on low for 3 hours. If you don't have a Crock-Pot, this can also simmer in a soup pot on the stove.

Add freshly cut "zoodles" or use gluten-free noodles to the finished soup to make a more filling dish.

Desserts and Breakfast

Apple Blueberry Crumble

4-5 servings

Since I have given up breads, cereals, and desserts, I wanted something sweet, but not too sweet for breakfast or even a treat after dinner.

Paired with fresh whipped cream it can be a dessert, or warm it up a little and serve with coconut cream for breakfast. You can add a little coconut sugar (¼ cup) to the crumble ingredients if you want to sweeten it more.

Get out these tools: mixing bowl, knives, cutting board, 8 x 8-inch pan

Crumble:

½ cup coconut oil, melted
¾ coconut flour
1 cup unsweetened shredded coconut
¼ tsp baking powder
¼ tsp baking soda
¼ tsp cardamom (use ½ tsp if you want a stronger cardamom flavor, but careful, this is a really intense spice)

Filling:

3 Granny Smith apples
¼ cup blueberries
1 tsp lemon juice
1 tbsp pure maple syrup

Mix the crumble ingredients together and set aside. Chop apples and pour into 8 x 8-inch baking pan along with blueberries. Add lemon juice and maple syrup. Pour crumble topping over apples and blueberries.

Bake at 350°F for 40 minutes.

Coconut Macaroons

makes about 12 cookies

How I love a good coconut macaroon! Since coconut is high in healthy fat and fiber, these little cookies will keep you full. I don't use much sugar in these at all, just a few drops of stevia extract. You can skip the stevia if you want the pure coconut flavor with no additional sweetness.

Get out these tools: mixing bowl, medium bowl, beaters, wooden spoon, cookie sheet, parchment paper

3 egg whites
5–10 drops of stevia extract
1 tsp vanilla extract
2½ cups unsweetened flaked coconut

Line cookie sheet with parchment paper. Preheat oven to 325°F.

With beaters, mix egg whites with stevia and vanilla until egg whites form peaks.

Add coconut and mix thoroughly.

Drop by rounded teaspoon on cookie sheet and bake for 20 minutes, until tops of cookies start to brown.

Dairy-Free Coconut Cream
with Protein Powder

1 serving

When faced with a strict anti-candida diet, eliminating all bread, cereal, waffles, muffins, and everything else I like to eat for breakfast, I had to get creative. What could be delicious and nutritious, but quick and easy?

This small bowl of coconut goodness keeps me full for hours thanks to the full fat of the coconut milk. I almost don't miss my favorite breakfast of peanut butter on toast. Almost.

Get out these tools: bowl and spoon

¾ cup unsweetened coconut flakes
½ cup of coconut cream (I prefer the Trader Joe's brand, which is creamy, not watery)
1 tsp protein powder★

Optional:
½ packet stevia or Monk fruit sweetener

Mix coconut with cream then sprinkle protein powder over top.

If you like a warmer oatmeal-type breakfast, mix the cream and coconut over a low flame in a small pot for a few minutes, and then sprinkle protein powder and sweetener over top.

NOTES

Coconut is a very low-oxalate food, and coconut cream is dairy free. If you are highly sensitive to oxalates, be careful with the Cacao Magic because it contains cacao, which is high in oxalates, I use it sparingly for a hint of flavor. Use a low-ox protein powder like Sprout Living Simple Pumpkin Seed Protein Powder instead of the Cacao Magic.

Or you can use chocolate extract in place of Cacao Magic, which is a low-oxalate option with chocolate flavor.

Sour Cream Coffee Cake
with Apricots

6-8 servings

Good news: Apricots are very low in oxalates! This coffee cake is delicious warm out of the oven and is perfect for breakfast or a snack. I'll warn you now that eating only one slice is a challenge, because it's so good.

There are numerous health benefits of apricots, one of my very favorite fruits. They are high in fiber and contain vitamins A and C as well as beta-carotene, potassium, and calcium.

Get out these tools: mixing bowls, beaters, Bundt pan

1 cup butter, melted
1 cup sugar, raw or coconut sugar
2 eggs
1 tsp vanilla
2 cups gluten-free flour
1½ tsp xanthan gum, only if gluten-free flour doesn't contain it
1½ tsp baking powder
¼ tsp baking soda
¼ tsp cardamom
1 cup sour cream
1 cup chopped apricots

Mix butter and sugar with beaters in a medium bowl. Add eggs and vanilla, mixing well.

In another bowl, mix the flour and dry ingredients then add slowly to the creamed sugar and butter. Add in sour cream and chopped apricots. Pour batter into a greased Bundt pan.

Bake at 350°F for 50 minutes.

> **NOTE**
>
> Just a reminder that not all gluten-free flours are low-oxalate. Always read ingredients.

Cherry Cobbler

4-5 servings

With many fruits and vegetables high in oxalates, I'm so grateful there are many tasty ones that fall into the low-oxalate category! Cherries are not only low in oxalates but are so good for you, containing antioxidants, vitamin C, and fiber.

Get out these tools: mixing bowls, 8 x 8-glassware or pan

Topping:
½ cup coconut flour
¼ cup melted coconut oil
1 cup shredded coconut
¼ cup coconut sugar

Filling:
1 tablespoon gelatin, unflavored
½ tsp nutmeg (1 tsp is medium oxalate, you can use nutmeg or cinnamon extract which is lower)
½ cup blueberries
½ cup cherries
pure maple syrup, optional

Combine topping in small bowl. In a separate bowl, stir together filling. Spoon topping over filling in pan and drizzle pure maple syrup to add sweetness, if desired.

Bake at 350°F for 25 minutes.

Coconut Vanilla Muffins

12 muffins

My favorite thing to eat in the morning is whatever is quick and easy. I love baking these muffins and eating them for breakfast along with a little coconut oil (instead of butter, though butter works just fine).

Get out these tools: mixing bowl, muffin tin

½ cup coconut flour
¼ tsp salt
¼ tsp baking soda
¼ cup coconut sugar
¼ unsweetened coconut flakes
4 eggs
⅓ cup milk (I use coconut milk)
½ tsp vanilla extract
3 tbsp pure maple syrup

Preheat oven to 350°F. Combine dry ingredients in medium bowl, and then stir in eggs, milk and vanilla. Spoon batter into lined muffin tins, half full. Drizzle with maple syrup, then another spoonful of batter, then another drizzle of syrup.

Bake for 22 minutes.

NOTES

Baking with coconut flour is something I do often since coconut is low in oxalates. You should know that the muffins or anything else you bake will be denser than a muffin made with traditional or even gluten-free flour.

Because the coconut flour is absorbent, you typically need more eggs to balance everything. Coconut flour contains a lot of fiber, and anything made with it will be filling.

Brunch Casserole

4-5 servings

I like serving up breakfast for dinner, and there was a time when I made this casserole every couple of weeks until my family got sick of it. I like the leftovers for my breakfast the next morning.

Popovers or muffins along with homemade applesauce rounds this out to be a good meal.

Get out these tools: mixing bowl, casserole dish

8 oz. turkey sausage, cooked and crumbled (buy in bulk form)
4 eggs, beaten
¾ cup cheddar cheese
1½ cup milk
1 cup shredded potatoes*, if tolerated
Salt and pepper, to taste

Preheat oven to 350°F. Spray 8-inch casserole pan with nonstick spray. I like avocado oil spray. Mix sausage, eggs, cheese, and milk in bowl, then pour into pan. Add potatoes if you wish. Sprinkle additional cheese on top and add salt and pepper.

Bake for 40 minutes.

NOTES

Additional add-ins: sautéed onions, zucchini, red peppers, broccoli (remember to boil broccoli first and use ½ cup, which is low-ox). Anything you can tolerate can be thrown into this casserole. I use cheddar cheese, but mozzarella works well too.

*A small piece (about a fourth) of a potato contains roughly 16 milligrams of oxalate, which might be tolerated if other ingredients are low or no oxalates. Red potatoes are lower in oxalates than white; ½ cup boiled without the skin is medium oxalate.

Low-Oxalate Breakfast Plate

1 serving

Sometimes I don't have muffins or egg cups ready but I need something to eat that's going to keep me full. I grab whatever I have handy and make a breakfast plate of low-oxalate foods.

I'll admit to adding a few homemade macaroons to my low-ox breakfast plate.

Get out these tools: knives, cutting board, plate

2–3 slices of crispy bacon
¼ cup sprouted pumpkin seeds
1 hard-boiled egg
sliced Granny Smith apples
small piece of cheddar cheese
sliced avocado
¼ cup ground beef, cooked

Arrange on a plate and enjoy this super simple low-oxalate plate that will keep you full for hours. The protein in the bacon, beef, cheese, and egg will give you energy along with the healthy fat in the avocado and pumpkin seeds. The apple gives the whole meal bit of sweetness.

Use any low-oxalate ingredients you have. When you're watching your oxalates, you really have to find ways to get creative and think outside of the box.

Ham and Egg Muffin Cups

makes 10 muffin cups

If you have silicone muffin liners, that makes cleanup a whole lot easier than having to scrub out muffin tins. You can prepare these a day ahead of time and store in the fridge.

Get out these tools: mixing bowl, muffin tin, knives, cutting board

4 eggs
¼ milk
½ cup mozzarella or cheddar cheese
½ cup ham, chopped
¼ cup chopped zucchini
salt and white pepper

Mix all ingredients in medium bowl, and then pour into greased muffin tins. Bake at 350°F for 20 to 25 minutes.

NOTE

Feel free to experiment and add in your favorite low-oxalate vegetables or spices. If you want to substitute ground beef, sausage, or turkey for the ham, you can do that too! I encourage you to use garlic and/or onion powder, or any spice you like.

Green Apple and Turkey Patties

makes 4-5 small patties

I like to make things ahead of time so I'm not cooking first thing in the morning. I highly recommend making these ahead of time, so in the morning, you can put one on a plate and heat it up quickly.

One of these and a muffin will hold you over until lunch. Or make a sandwich out of the patties by putting them on gluten-free buns or rolls. You can use low-oxalate coconut wraps too.

Get out these tools: mixing bowl, knives, cutting board, skillet

1 lb. ground turkey
½ cup small green apple, chopped
1 egg
1 tbsp coconut flour
½ tsp onion powder
½ tsp dried sage
½ tsp thyme
1 tsp maple syrup
1 tbsp coconut oil for pan

Combine all ingredients except oil in a medium bowl. Melt coconut oil in a pan over medium heat. While oil is melting, form turkey mixture into patties. Cook 2 to 3 minutes on each side, flipping over until cooked through.

Season with salt and pepper to taste.

NOTE

I made these without the apple and discovered that my dogs really like these too.

No-Grain Granola

makes about 3 servings

One of the things I miss most while watching oxalates is a good granola. Cereal used to be one of my favorite breakfast foods and I've been searching high and low for a low-oxalate version.

Many store-bought granolas are high in white processed sugar, which I try hard to avoid, and they also include nuts. If you are skipping grains and watching your sugar intake, granola is something you may not be able to enjoy.

I came up with this No-Grain Granola as an alternative. It's easy and quick to make, low in sugar, and has no grains. There are also options to add other things to give it more substance and excitement!

Get out these tools: mixing bowl, parchment paper, cookie sheet

2 tbsp of coconut flour
⅓ cup coconut sugar, or ten drops of stevia extract
½ cup coconut oil, melted
½ tsp vanilla
1 tsp nutmeg (mace is a good low-oxalate substitute or you can use extracts)
3 cups shredded, unsweetened coconut flakes

Preheat oven to 350°F. Mix all ingredients in medium bowl and spread out on parchment-lined cookie sheet. Bake at 350°F and stir frequently with wooden spoon, making sure coconut browns evenly. Once coconut is light brown and toasted, remove from oven, about 10 minutes.

NOTES

You can add raisins, sprouted pumpkin seeds, or dried apples to this to make it a little more substantial.

Want to add oats? ½ cup

Total Oxalate Value: 16.66 mg
Soluble Oxalates: 9.98 mg

Low-Sugar Banana Bread

makes one loaf, about six servings

I love banana bread! It's good as a dessert or breakfast, and works with coffee or tea. Makes a great snack. The natural sweetness of the bananas eliminates the need for a lot of sugar. I do add a little organic, non-GMO coconut sugar.

Bananas are medium-oxalate so I only make this bread once in a while. While they do not bother me cooked, I cannot eat them raw. Take notes on how you feel after eating this bread.

Get out these tools: mixing bowl, beaters, glass loaf pan

¼–½ cup coconut sugar, depending on how sweet you want the bread
½ coconut oil
2 eggs
2 mashed ripe bananas
½ cup low-sugar applesauce
1 tsp vanilla
1½ cup gluten-free flour
1 tsp baking soda
1tsp xanthan gum

Preheat oven to 350°F. Mix sugar and oil with eggs then add mashed bananas, applesauce, and vanilla in medium/large bowl. Slowly add flour, baking soda, and xanthan gum.

Pour into loaf pan that has been lightly greased with coconut oil. Bake at 350°F for 50 minutes.

NOTES

1 raw banana:

Total Oxalate Value: 8.02 mg
Soluble Oxalates: 0.83 mg

Gluten-Free Crepes

makes 5 crepes

For making crepes, a nonstick ceramic skillet works best. I have a medium ceramic skillet, and the fact that it's nonstick makes it very easy to get a spatula under the crepe and flip it.

You can fill these with savory or sweet filling, eat them alone like a pancake, or add fruit.

Get out these tools: mixing bowl, nonstick ceramic skillet

1 cup gluten-free flour
2 cups coconut milk (add a little more if batter is too thick)
2 eggs
2 tbsp coconut oil

1 tsp vanilla or vanilla bean powder (I like the Bulletproof vanilla bean powder)
If you want the crepes to be sweeter, add a few drops of stevia extract

In a medium bowl, use a whisk to blend ingredients.

Using the nonstick ceramic skillet, spread batter evenly on bottom. Batter should be thin but not runny. One cup of batter makes one crepe. Batter will bubble when it's time to turn crepe over. Cook on both sides, using spatula to carefully flip crepe over.

Peaches with Cardamom

makes enough to fill 2-3 crepes

These go perfectly with the crepes or the No-Grain Granola. They are also tasty with coconut cream or yogurt. Peaches are a low-oxalate fruit, and cardamom is a low-oxalate alternative to high-oxalate cinnamon.

Like nutmeg, cardamom is a very strong spice, so you don't need much. It's used a lot in Indian cuisine and was used as a treatment in ancient medicine. An old folk remedy uses cardamom to cure hiccups!

Get out these tools: small soup pan

¾ cup peaches (I used frozen organic peaches, defrosted)
¼–½ tsp cardamom
1 scoop collagen powder
½ tsp raw honey

Over low heat, mix all ingredients until warm and heated through.

Desserts and Breakfast

99

Turkey Sausage Hash

2-3 servings

There was once a time when I could eat anything I wanted. My favorite breakfast was peanut butter on toast—if there is one food that I miss, it's peanut butter. Unfortunately, peanut butter (along with other nut butters) is high-oxalate, and I avoid eating it.

I have had to get creative for breakfast—which everyone knows is an important start to the day.

This hash is full of nutrients and protein and can be made ahead of time. It's good on its own or with a muffin.

Get out these tools: mixing bowl, knives, cutting board, skillet

8 ounces of turkey sausage
1 tsp coconut oil
1 tsp onion powder
½ cup butternut squash, chopped and cooked
½ zucchini, chopped and cooked
pure maple syrup
salt + white pepper

In a large skillet, cook sausage in coconut oil until no longer pink. Add onion powder, squash, and zucchini, mixing thoroughly. When heated through, finish with a light drizzle of pure maple syrup. Season with salt and white pepper to taste.

Apple Muffins

makes 12 muffins

Coconut flour baked goods are dense, but these are light and soft. I like using butter rather than coconut oil, because I love a hint of buttery flavor, but you can use either.

Get out these tools: mixing bowl, beaters, muffin tins

1 cup applesauce (unsweetened, organic)
4 eggs
¼ cup melted butter (you can use coconut oil if you prefer)
2 tbsp maple syrup or ¼ cup coconut sugar
1 tsp vanilla extract
1 cup coconut flour
1 tsp baking soda
1 tsp baking powder

Line muffin tins with liners. Combine applesauce, eggs, butter, maple syrup (if using instead of coconut sugar), and vanilla, then add in dry ingredients, stirring well. Pour batter into tins and bake at 350°F for 20 minutes.

Cranberry Loaf

6 servings

So many paleo and gluten-free recipes call for almond flour, which is very high in oxalates. I strictly avoid it. It's such a letdown to find an awesome-sounding recipe and see that it calls for almond flour. And almond flour and coconut flour are not interchangeable. Other gluten-free flours tend to be high in oxalates, like cassava and plantain flours.

Adjust your expectations when baking with coconut flour and know your breads and muffins will be slightly denser and thicker. I'd love to find a good low-oxalate flour that is easy to bake with. Until then, I mostly use coconut flour and sometimes, the gluten-free flour blends I mention in the beginning of this book.

Get out these tools: mixing bowl, beaters, loaf pan

6 eggs
2 tbsp melted coconut oil
¾ cup coconut milk
1 tsp vanilla extract
⅔ cup coconut flour
1 tsp baking soda
¼ cup coconut sugar
¾ cup cranberries, fresh

Mix eggs, oil, milk, and vanilla together in a large bowl. In a separate bowl, combine flour, baking soda, and sugar. Add dry ingredients to wet ingredients and stir in cranberries.

Pour into a greased loaf pan and bake for 1 hour at 350°F or until bread is cooked through and browned on top.

Mango Granola Parfait

1-2 servings

Mangos are high in vitamins C, B6, A, E, and K. They also offer up fiber, selenium, calcium, and iron. They are also low in oxalates and are delicious! You can buy them fresh or frozen in chunks. For this recipe I used fresh mango.

Get out these tools: small mixing bowl, knife, serving dish

½ cup coconut cream
½ cup mango, cubed
½ cup No-Grain Granola
5 drops of stevia extract
½ tsp of vanilla extract

Mix coconut cream, mango, stevia, and vanilla in a bowl. Layer the granola with the coconut cream then top with granola and repeat.

NOTE

You can use vanilla yogurt instead of the coconut cream, but the coconut cream is dairy free. Due to the histamines in yogurt, I skip it in favor of the full-fat coconut cream.

Snacks, Sides, Drinks, and Miscellaneous

Bladder-Soothing Smoothie

1 serving

If you suffer from interstitial cystitis (painful bladder disease) then this low-oxalate, soothing drink might give you a little relief. Cucumbers are cooling, and aloe is healing.

Cucumbers are also low in calories and high in water content, vitamin K, and B vitamins. They contain anti–inflammatory properties.

Get out these tools: knife, cutting board, blender

½ cup chopped cucumber
¼ cup cilantro
1 small green apple, cut into pieces
1 tbsp of aloe vera gel or juice
1 cup water

Blend all in a Vitamix (or powerful blender) until smooth.

Mango Smoothie

1 serving

Naturally sweet, this mango smoothie is a great snack. It's thick and filling, which makes it a perfect mid-morning or mid-afternoon treat to keep you full until your next meal.

Skip the raw honey if you don't like your smoothies sweet.

Get out these tools: knife, cutting board, blender

½ cup mango
1 cup coconut milk
½ tbsp raw honey
½ tsp vanilla extract

Mix in blender on high until smooth.

NOTES

A standard smoothie recipe is 1 cup of liquid, ½ cup of fresh or frozen fruit. Add protein powder, as tolerated. You can add flax, which is low in oxalate. Resist the temptation to add chia seeds; they are high in oxalate! I wanted to add them to everything until I learned this.

Pineapple Ginger Smoothie

1 serving, medium oxalate

Pineapple is very healing thanks to bromelain, an enzyme that is anti-inflammatory. Pineapple also contains 130 percent of the daily requirement of vitamin C. This tropical fruit is full of thiamin, folates, pyridoxine, biotin, riboflavin, copper, and potassium.

Ginger has enormous medicinal properties. It's long been used in medicine and is recommended for nausea and pain reduction. Ginger contains anti-diabetic properties and helps with indigestion and cancer prevention.

Get out these tools: knife, cutting board, blender

½ cup pineapple cut into chunks
small piece of ginger (1 tbsp fresh ginger is medium-oxalate; I use less than ½ tbsp)
½ cup shredded coconut
1 cup water
1 scoop collagen powder

Mix on high in blender until smooth.

NOTE

You can use ginger extract for the flavor and none of the oxalates.

1 teaspoon of fresh ginger

Total Oxalate Value: 3.48 mg

Soluble Oxalates: 3.48 mg

Mango Coconut Smoothie

1 serving

This smoothie is tropical and tasty. It's low in oxalates, high in fiber, and low in sugar. It's also pretty filling, so it makes a great addition to breakfast and will keep you full for a long time.

Get out these tools: knife, cutting board, blender

2 cups mango, cut into pieces
¼ cup coconut chunks (I buy frozen coconut chunks)
½ tbsp honey
½ tsp vanilla extract
1 cup coconut milk

Blend in blender until smooth, and drink right away.

Watermelon Cucumber Smoothie

1 serving

Watermelon is a powerhouse fruit. Not only is it low in oxalates and naturally sweet but it's high in vitamins A, B6, and C. It is also high in water content, which is excellent for hydration, plus it contains lycopene, a compound that fights cancer.

Get out these tools: knife, cutting board, blender

1 cup watermelon chunks
½ cup cucumber pieces
1 tbsp mint
1 tbsp aloe gel
½ cup water

Add all ingredients to blender and mix well.

Watermelon Basil Strawberry Smoothie

1 serving

Watermelon is low in oxalates, as is basil. Fresh basil contains anti-inflammatory properties, protects the liver, boosts the immune system, and also contains antibacterial compounds. This smoothie is savory rather than supersweet.

Sometimes I react to strawberries, even though they are low-oxalate per half cup. I try to watch the oxalate content of what I eat (more so than usual) after drinking this smoothie.

Get out these tools: knife, cutting board, blender

1 cup chunks of watermelon
½ cup strawberries
½ cup water
1 tsp fresh basil
½ juice from lime

Blend all ingredients in a food processor or blender until well combined.

NOTES

Strawberries are low-oxalate per half cup. The peels of lemons, limes, and oranges are high-oxalate, so be sure you are not ingesting any peel!

½ cup of strawberries

Total Oxalate Value: 2.20 mg

Soluble Oxalates: 0.68 mg

Ranch-Seasoned Carrots

4 servings

For the longest time I made carrots one way and only one way. With butter, brown sugar, and a dash of cinnamon. Then I switched to coconut oil and coconut sugar. Now I make them with herbs, and it's become my favorite way to cook them.

Get out these tools: knife, cutting board, cookie sheet

16 oz. carrots (I used organic, medium-size carrots from Trader Joe's, which I boiled before roasting)
¼ tsp dill
½ tsp onion powder
½ tsp garlic powder
2 tbsp parsley, dried
½ tsp white pepper
½ tsp salt
2 tbsp olive oil

Preheat oven to 400°F. Mix all the ingredients, except the oil, in a bowl and make sure carrots are coated thoroughly. Spread on cookie sheet and drizzle with the olive oil.

Bake at 400°F for about 20 to 25 minutes until carrots are roasted.

NOTES

Carrots are one of those nutrient-packed vegetables that people love. Unfortunately they contain medium levels of oxalates. You may think you have to give them up completely, but you don't!

The good news is that boiling helps decrease the oxalate content. The bad news is boiling doesn't eliminate the oxalates completely. If you're avoiding medium- to high-oxalate foods, you might want to skip carrots completely.

Boil carrots for ten minutes, them drain and follow the directions to roast. Instead of cooking for 20 minutes in the oven, decrease the oven time so carrots don't get too soft.

½ cup of boiled carrots

Total Oxalate Value: 3.82 mg

Soluble Oxalates: 1.79 mg

Snacks, Sides, Drinks, and Miscellaneous

Sautéed Bok Choy

3-4 servings

Bok choy used to be one of those vegetables I'd pass in the grocery store because I was not sure what to do with it, so I kept walking. Much like radishes.

I wonder what else I'm missing out on?

I started throwing bok choy in stir-fry dishes and now I make it as an easy side dish. This is a cruciferous vegetable and contains anticancer properties. You will find vitamins A and C, beta-carotene, selenium, iron, and zinc in bok choy.

Get out these tools: knives, cutting board, skillet

2 bok choy, chopped
2 tbsp olive or avocado oil
1 tsp chopped garlic
½ tsp Himalayan salt
½ tsp white pepper

Slice bok choy into pieces, removing stem. Heat oil in a pan or skillet then add garlic. Add the bok choy and sauté over medium-high heat. Stir evenly for 4 to 5 minutes. Add salt and white pepper to taste.

Zoodles/Zucchini Noodles

2-3 servings

If you don't have a spiralizer, I highly recommend one for these zoodles! I bought mine for under twenty dollars, and it's great to have on hand for when I want to create noodles from zucchini. You can also spiralize yellow squash, apples, cucumber, and more. Have fun and experiment with any low-oxalate vegetable.

Zucchini noodles are my favorite substitute for pasta noodles. Look at how easy these are to make!

Get out this tool: spiralizer

1–2 medium-size zucchini
1 tsp of sea salt

Run zucchini through the spiralizer until every piece is cut into a spiral. Set zoodles on a paper towel and sprinkle sea salt over zoodles.

Allow them to sit for at least ten minutes, then blot with a paper towel. Serve raw or lightly heat in a pan with olive oil. Don't overcook or they will turn mushy.

You can use these zoodles in place of most noodles, like in the Herbed Chicken Soup.

Cucumber Salad

1-2 servings

Are you a big fan of cucumbers like I am? I like them in a salad or as a snack and one of my favorites is to slice them and sprinkle with Himalayan salt.

If I have the time, I'll make this side dish which is simple and can easily be adjusted for your own specific preferences. Skip the vinegar if you aren't a fan of acid, or leave off the stevia if you don't want the sweetness.

Get out these tools: knife, cutting board, small bowl

½ tsp Himalayan salt
2 tbsp olive oil
1 tbsp apple cider vinegar
3 drops stevia extract
juice from ½ lemon
2–3 Persian cucumbers cut into pieces
white pepper, to taste

Mix salt, oil, vinegar, stevia, lemon juice together with a whisk in a bowl, and then pour over cucumbers. Add white pepper to suit taste.

NOTES

If you want this simple cucumber dish to have a little zing, add ½ teaspoon of red pepper flakes. Skip the stevia if you don't want the sweetness. Red pepper flakes are low-oxalate per teaspoon. 1 tablespoon of crushed red pepper flakes is low ox. Apple cider vinegar is very low in oxalates per teaspoon.

Gluten-Free Popovers

makes 12 popovers

What a great little side dish instead of bread or rolls! Made with gluten-free flour, these are fast and easy. They pair well with the Herbed Chicken Soup or any of the soups in this book. Best served warm out of the oven with a little dab of butter or ghee.

Get out these tools: mixing bowl, beaters, muffin tin

1 cup gluten-free flour blend
½ tsp xanthan gum (if you use Better Batter flour, you don't need xanthan gum)
2 eggs, beaten
1 tbsp butter
1 cup milk, low fat organic

Mix together dry ingredients in medium bowl then add eggs, melted butter, and milk. Mix well but don't overmix.

Pour batter into greased muffin tins and cook for 20 minutes at 400°F. Poke a hole (I use knife tip), on top of popover, then bake for 10 more minutes.

NOTES

Always check flour blends before you bake. Keep in mind that even gluten-free flour can be high-oxalate. I'd love to find a low-oxalate flour, if you have one, let me know!

Better Batter contains the following: rice flour, brown rice flour, tapioca starch, potato starch, potato flour, xanthan gum, pectin.

Snacks, Sides, Drinks, and Miscellaneous

Cauliflower Rice

3-4 servings

Like zoodles, cauliflower rice is versatile and can be used in place of white rice or pasta. You can make the rice and freeze in ziplock bags or you can buy premade cauliflower rice to save time.

Get out these tools: knife, cutting board, food processor, plastic ziplock bag to store extra

1 head of cauliflower
1 tbsp of olive oil or coconut oil
salt + white pepper

Wash cauliflower and remove stem and green leaves. Chop roughly into pieces and run pieces through a food processor until pieces become small.

To cook, heat olive oil or coconut oil in skillet and cook until heated through and slightly softened.

Add salt and pepper to taste.

Snacks, Sides, Drinks, and Miscellaneous

Green Beans & Bacon

4 servings, medium-oxalate per serving

What you'll want to know about green beans is that they are moderate in oxalates; I cook them once in a while as a side dish. If you are aiming to consume 40 to 50 mg each day of oxalates, in the green beans you will find 10–25mg (per ½ cup).

They are high in fiber and dense in vitamins such as A, C, K, and B6. They also contain calcium and folic acid.

I like fresh green beans, but if they aren't available, frozen is next best and I always boil them. Boiling reduces soluble oxalate content, but does not remove oxalates completely. They are medium to very high in oxalate depending on variety.

Green beans with a little salt and pepper is the easiest side dish, a little drizzle of fresh lemon juice brings out the flavor.

For a more substantial side dish, add a bit of crumbled bacon. I like these beans with the meatloaf I make; the flavors really complement each other.

Get out these tools: skillet, cookie sheet, aluminum foil, knife, cutting board

3–4 slice of bacon plus bacon grease
3 cups green beans, I like frozen green beans (already cleaned and ends snipped off)
½ tsp garlic powder
salt + pepper

Brown bacon using oven and cookie sheet method below. Pour off bacon grease into glass bowl.

Sauté green beans until cooked (about ten minutes) using one tablespoon of bacon grease in skillet. Season with garlic powder, salt, and pepper.

Chop cooked bacon into crumbles and sprinkle over green beans. You can also add gluten-free fried onions to the beans and bacon.

*Cookie sheet cooking method: line cookie sheet with aluminum foil, spread out bacon on sheet. Set oven to 425°F and stick bacon in oven. Bacon will slowly cook while oven is heating. When oven has reached 425°F, bacon will be cooked. Remove from oven and pour off grease. I save bacon grease for cooking at a later time. Blot bacon with paper towels to remove excess grease.

I like no-sugar, no-nitrates, no-antibiotics bacon.

> **NOTES**
>
> Different varieties of green beans equal different oxalate counts. String beans are 9mg per half cup.
>
> **½ cup boiled green beans**
>
> Total Oxalate Value: 19.53 mg
>
> Soluble Oxalates: 9.73 mg

Tzatziki Sauce

makes about 1 cup of sauce

Before I was watching oxalates and avoiding gluten, I used to go to a restaurant that served amazing Greek food including garlicky tzatziki sauce that I could practically eat with a fork by itself!

Unfortunately I determined the food there was loaded with gluten. From then on, I was unable to enjoy visiting and had to figure out how to make their sauce at home. This one is tasty, and I make it with lots of garlic and salt. I eat it with gluten-free crackers or over baked chicken.

Get out these tools: knife, cutting board, food processor, mixing bowl, strainer

1 cucumber
1 tbsp fresh dill, chopped
1 tbsp minced garlic
1 tbsp olive oil
½ cup sour cream
juice of ½ lemon (about 1 tbsp)
salt and pepper

Run cucumber through food processor so the cucumber is chopped finely. Put cucumber in strainer and drain the excess water. I used a cloth to squeeze water. This helps the sauce remain thick, not watery.

Add cucumber to bowl and mix in all other ingredients. Adjust the lemon and salt to taste.

NOTE

An important step here is to drain the water from the cucumber. If you skip this step, the sauce will be thin and watery.

Roasted Red Pepper Sauce

makes about 1 cup of sauce

This is for those who cannot tolerate tomatoes at all. Tomatoes are tricky since fresh tomatoes are medium-oxalate, but canned are high-oxalate and different varieties of tomatoes vary. Roasted red pepper sauce is a good alternative and a better lower-oxalate option.

Get out these tools: knife, cutting board, soup pot, immersion blender, cookie sheet

5 fresh red peppers
¼ cup olive oil
1–2 tsp garlic power
1 tsp thyme
1 tsp basil
½ tsp salt
½ tsp white pepper

Set oven to broil. While it's heating, clean peppers and slice into halves. Clean out the seeds. Lay on cookie sheet and allow peppers to roast, about 5–10 minutes or until peppers start to blacken.

Remove peppers from oven, run under cold water, and peel the skin. Chop into pieces and add to a pot with the ¼ cup of olive oil. Set heat to medium. With a wooden spoon, stir and allow the peppers to soften.

When the peppers are soft, use an immersion blender to liquefy. Add more olive oil if the sauce is too thick. Add spices and allow the sauce to simmer for ten minutes, stirring.

NOTES

I had to adjust my taste buds a little. This is not anything like tomato sauce (slightly sweeter) so don't expect it to be identical to a marinara sauce. It works really well on pasta and zoodles, and the taste goes nicely with meatballs.

Avocado Dressing

Thank goodness for avocados. With a very restricted diet of no sugars, yeast, gluten, soy, and more, I add avocado to whatever I can but not too much because they are high in histamines. I started eating avocados fairly recently when it was determined that I'd have to really watch what I ate and I felt like I couldn't eat much of anything.

Avocados can be eaten with eggs at breakfast, in a salad at lunch, and added to whatever you eat for dinner. With a little salt and pepper, they are tasty by themselves.

This dressing gives a little weight to a simple salad of romaine lettuce, red cabbage, and cucumbers.

Get out these tools: knife, cutting board, mixing bowl, whisk

1 ripe avocado
1 tbsp garlic powder
3 tbsp of olive oil
¼ cup sour cream
juice from ½ lemon
½ tsp salt
¼ tsp white pepper

Mix ingredients in a blender until combined and smooth. Whisk in more oil or 1 tablespoon of water if it's too thick.

Lemon Dressing

makes enough for 3-4 salads

A simple, light dressing that is suitable over any kind of lettuce. If you are watching your oxalates closely, you will want to stick with romaine or iceberg.

Get out these tools: knife, cutting board, mixing bowl, whisk, and immersion blender

½ cup juice from two lemons
1 garlic clove, chopped
½ cup olive or avocado oil

Optional:
3 tsp of spicy brown mustard

Whisk or blend until completely emulsified.

Buttermilk Ranch Dressing

makes enough for 4 salads

When you see how easy this is to make, you will never buy processed ranch dressing again.

Buy a carton of buttermilk and use for this dressing and use whatever is left over to marinate the chicken in the buttermilk chicken recipe.

Get out these tools: knife, cutting board, mixing bowl, whisk

1 tsp dill
1 tsp chives
1 tsp garlic powder
1 tsp onion powder
1 tsp salt
1 tsp pepper

½ tsp lemon juice
½ tsp olive oil
½ cup buttermilk
¼ cup mayonnaise
½ cup sour cream

Thoroughly whisk all ingredients together in medium bowl until well blended.

NOTE

This dressing is the perfect dipping sauce for the Fried Zucchini!

Simple Spiced Apples

What can you do when you want something sweet but you have to watch your sugar intake and/or oxalates? After you dry your tears, you turn to apples!

I've always loved apple pie, and the best part for me is the inside. The flavor combination of tart Granny Smith apples with a hint of vanilla, combined with a little coconut cream, is a healthy treat to eat for dessert or breakfast.

Get out these tools: knife, cutting board, pot

2 cups of water
3 Granny Smith apples, chopped into medium-size chunks
¼ teaspoon vanilla
10 drops of stevia extract
1 tsp of nutmeg (mace is a lower oxalate option)
cinnamon extract (low in oxalate), if desired, to taste

Bring water to a boil on stovetop; add apple pieces, vanilla, stevia drops. Turn heat to medium-low. Allow apples to soften, about ten minutes.

When apples are soft, drain water. Pour apples into a bowl or container. sprinkle with nutmeg, mace, or cinnamon extract. Serve warm with a spoonful of coconut cream, if desired.

NOTES

I eat these for breakfast, as a snack, anytime really. If you are missing the combination of apples and cinnamon, which go together like peanut butter and jelly, then go for the cinnamon extract for flavor.

If you really want to use cinnamon, consider the oxalate count.

1 teaspoon of ground cinnamon

Total Oxalate Value: 33.50 mg

Soluble Oxalates: 2.54 mg

138

Oven-Baked Onion Rings

3-4 servings

As the only one in my family who has to be gluten-free and low-oxalate, I get very envious of my family as they enjoy things like French fries and onion rings. Sometimes I tear up a little thinking about all of the foods I can't eat.

However, I have discovered I can eat onion rings if I make them myself. These are best right out of the oven.

Get out these tools: knife, cutting board, mixing bowls, foil lined cookie sheet

avocado oil nonstick spray
1 large sweet onion, sliced into rings about ½-inch think
1 cup gluten-free bread crumbs
1 tbsp garlic powder
2 eggs + 3 tbsp water
½ cup Bobs Red Mill One to One Flour (keep in mind this flour hasn't been tested so I don't know the oxalate content)
salt and pepper to taste

Preheat oven to 450°F. Line cookie sheet with foil and spray with nonstick spray.

Soak rings in water or milk for ten minutes; this helps mellow out the sharp bite of the onion.

Pour gluten-free bread crumbs into a bowl and add garlic powder. Combine. Lightly beat eggs plus water in another bowl. Flour in a third bowl.

Coat rings in flour, then dip in egg mixture, then dip in bread crumbs and place on cookie sheet.

Bake at 450°F for 10 to 15 minutes until browned.

Remove from oven and sprinkle with salt and pepper.

NOTES

These baked onion rings pair nicely with meatloaf. I like onion rings with either BBQ sauce or my homemade Buttermilk Ranch dressing.

Deviled Eggs with Avocado

2-3 servings

This is another recipe where there's not a whole lot of cooking to be done. This one calls on you to assemble, rather than cook. Use any leftover bacon you might have, and feel free to add more than what is called for here.

Get out these tools: knife, cutting board, mixing bowl

3 hard-boiled eggs
½ avocado
¼ cup avocado mayonnaise or Vegenaise
1 tsp garlic powder
1–2 pieces of crisp bacon, crumbled into small pieces
½ tsp salt
¼ tsp cayenne pepper (use Tabasco for more of a kick)

Slice eggs in half and scoop yolks into a bowl. Add avocado, mayo, garlic powder, bacon pieces, and salt then mix well.

Spoon mixture into eggs and sprinkle lightly with cayenne pepper.

NOTE

The best way to hard-boil eggs: put eggs in pot, add water. Bring water to a boil then cover and remove from heat. Let the eggs sit covered in hot water for ten minutes. Eggs will be perfectly hard-boiled!

Garlic Roasted Radishes

1-2 servings

Radishes are one of those vegetables that I used to see in the produce section (like the bok choy) and think, "Meh, no thanks," and keep moving. But when I had to go on a low-oxalate diet (more like low-oxalate way of living), I needed to consider using a variety of low-oxalate vegetables. I had to go beyond my standard cucumbers and romaine lettuce routine.

I saw a recipe for zucchini chips and figured I could swap out the zucchini and use radishes and wow, these turned out really good! After making these, I won't be skipping the radish section any more.

Radishes are not only low in oxalates, but contain fiber, riboflavin, potassium, plus copper, vitamin B6, magnesium, manganese, and calcium. There are a lot of nutrients packed into these edible little root vegetables.

Get out these tools: knife, cutting board, aluminum-foil-lined cookie sheet

1 bunch of radishes, cleaned with stems cut off
1 tsp dill
1 tsp onion powder
1 tsp garlic powder
1 tsp chopped dill
¼ cup olive oil

Thinly slice a bunch of radishes. One bunch will probably be about ten radishes. The thinner you can slice them, the crispier they will be after they are cooked.

Mix spices in a bowl. Spread out the radishes on a foil-lined cookie sheet and drizzle with olive oil. Be sure to coat all pieces. Sprinkle spices over radish slices.

Bake for 20 minutes at 450°F or until radishes are crispy.

NOTE

Confession: I ate the entire pan of radishes after I made them and took photos of them. The oil and spices combine well with the natural peppery flavor of the radishes, and this is a whole new way to consume a low-oxalate vegetable that is very nutritious. The crispy ones reminded me of potato chips, which I don't eat due to oxalates.

Mexican Spiced Corn

3-4 servings

This goes nicely with the Mexican Beef Wrap, keeping all the flavors in the same family. The cotija cheese adds a salty flavor so you don't need any extra salt. Unless you want it, of course.

Get out these tools: skillet, knife, cutting board

1 tbsp avocado oil
1 can of corn (9.2 ounces, I like the corn from Trader Joe's)
¼ tsp cayenne pepper
1 tsp Mexican seasoning (the Spice Hunter Mexican blend hasn't been tested for oxalates)
⅓ cup chopped cilantro
2 tbsp of cotija cheese
juice from ½ lime

Heat oil in skillet; add corn and spices on low heat. Lightly warm up the corn. Remove from heat and add cilantro, cheese, and lime juice.

If you are making this ahead of time, hold off on adding cilantro and lime so flavors are fresh.

NOTE

Turn this into a main course by adding chopped ground beef, romaine lettuce, roasted red peppers, and sliced avocado. Adjust the cayenne pepper as needed.

Watermelon Salsa

2-4 servings

I was trying to figure out what to do with my leftover watermelon and came up with this salsa, which is also like a little salad or even a little something you can serve on the side of a fancier dish.

The flavors are so bright and tasty! Feel free to add more mint and orange juice to suit your preferences. After I made this, I spooned it over some romaine lettuce and ate the whole thing.

Get out these tools: small bowl, medium bowl, knife, cutting board

¼ cup avocado oil
juice from ½ orange
½ cucumber, cut into small pieces
½ small watermelon, cut into pieces
1 tbsp chopped fresh mint

Combine oil plus juice in a small bowl. In a medium bowl, mix cucumber, watermelon, and mint. Drizzle juice mixture over watermelon and cucumber.

NOTES

I wanted to use lime juice as the main citrus juice in the dressing but I only had oranges so I used that and liked the flavor. The mint gives a burst of freshness and the watermelon is naturally sweet and the cucumber crisp and clean. This can be thrown together quickly and goes well with the Mexican Beef Wrap and Mexican Spiced Corn.

Roasted Cauliflower

3-4 servings

During my whole childhood and into my adult years, I did not like cauliflower. At all. While I still do not like broccoli, I have changed my tune with cauliflower. It was only fairly recently that I began experimenting with it because there wasn't much else I could safely eat. Now I like this cancer-fighting vegetable and eat it weekly.

Cauliflower is also good raw, dipped in a little buttermilk dressing.

Get out these tools: knife, cutting board, bowl, cookie sheet lined with aluminum foil

1 head of cauliflower
¼ cup olive oil
1 tsp minced garlic
1 tsp paprika (medium-oxalate)
1 tsp onion powder
1 cup Parmesan cheese
¼ cup gluten-free panko bread crumbs (hasn't been tested, use Rice Chex in place of the panko)

Preheat oven to 400°F. Clean and cut cauliflower florets into large pieces. Toss with oil and spices, spread on cookie sheet and roast for twenty minutes at 400°F or until browned and completely cooked.

NOTE

1 teaspoon of paprika

Total Oxalate Value: 5.68 mg

Soluble Oxalates: 3.24 mg

Bacon Chips and Easy Guacamole

1-2 servings

Bacon and avocado make a great combination here. This is the perfect mid-afternoon snack! You've got your delicious bacon paired with a smooth guacamole, and the whole thing gives you protein and fat for energy.

The turkey bacon cooks up without shrinking, unlike pork bacon, which reduces in size.

When you cut the turkey bacon into squares, it makes a nice chip. You get good fats and nutrients from the avocado and protein from the turkey bacon.

Get out these tools: knife, cutting board, small bowl, cookie sheet lined with aluminum foil

1 package of nitrite-free, sugar-free uncured turkey bacon
1 avocado
1 tsp salsa (I like Trader Joe's salsa, mild)
lime juice from ¼ lime
½ tsp salt

To make the turkey bacon, line cookie sheet with aluminum, cut bacon into squares (I used my kitchen scissors) and place bacon pieces evenly on cookie sheets.

Turn oven to 425°F and place bacon in oven. It will slowly cook as oven heats. When temperature has reached 425°F, bacon will be cooked or let it go a little longer to crisp up more.

To make the guacamole, slice avocado in half and squeeze insides into a bowl. Add 1 teaspoon of salsa, lime, and salt. Mix until smooth.

Homemade Tomato Sauce

Fresh tomatoes contain only a moderate level of oxalates, or between 2 and 10 mg per serving. I love tomatoes; this sauce is a delicious treat and goes well with meatballs and zoodles.

I am including this sauce for those who can tolerate tomatoes, but fear not if you have to skip it, because I made a roasted red pepper sauce for you. Since tomatoes are my "once in a while" food, I can eat this without a problem. I won't be offended if you don't try this sauce. If you cannot tolerate tomatoes, it's best you don't make it.

It's definitely not low-oxalate, especially with the crushed and Roma tomatoes which are high-oxalate. Oxalates might be medium per serving depending on the number of servings.

Get out these tools: knife, cutting board, Dutch oven (very large pot), potato masher or large wooden spoon

½ cup olive oil, plus additional teaspoon
8 Roma tomatoes, washed and cut into chunks
1 28-oz. can of crushed tomatoes
1 tbsp minced garlic
2 tbsp onion powder
¼ teaspoon anise
1 tsp salt
fresh basil

In a large soup pot/Dutch oven, pour ½ cup olive oil and roughly cut tomatoes, set heat on medium low and cook, stirring occasionally, until tomatoes are soft. When they are soft, use the back of a wooden spoon or potato masher to break up tomatoes.

Once tomatoes are broken up, pour in 28 oz. of crushed tomatoes and turn heat to low. Add minced garlic, onion powder, pinch of anise, salt and pepper plus one teaspoon of olive oil and stir. Let this simmer on low for 3 to 4 hours. Excess liquid will simmer off and sauce will thicken.

I add several torn leaves of fresh basil at the end of cooking for a little extra flavor.

NOTES

Some tomatoes contain only a moderate level of oxalates, or between 2 and 10 mg per serving. ½ cup of Big Beef or Brandywine tomatoes are low-oxalate.

Quick Hummus

6-8 servings

When I learned garbanzo beans were low-oxalate, it was a total game changer! After staying far away from hummus, I grew so excited to learn I could have it again. I think I might explode when I can eat a chocolate chip cookie. Food has become such a source of anxiety and joy for me since my health issues.

But I digress! I made this hummus and it was really good, I served it up on turkey patties (the ones from this cookbook) leaving out the green apple.

2 (15.5-oz.) cans garbanzo beans (Trader Joe's)
2 tsp olive oil, keep oil nearby because you will be adding more (probably ¼ cup total)
2–3 tbsp of garlic powder
1½ tsp onion powder
juice from ½ lemon
1 tsp salt or more if you want it, I like things salty
¼ cup jarred roasted red peppers plus 1–2 tsp of juice

Rinse and drain both cans of garbanzo beans. Pour into food processor, add olive oil and spices. Turn food processor on high. If the beans get stuck, add a little more olive oil. When beans are beginning to smooth, add red peppers and the juice from the jar along with juice from ½ lemon. Turn the food processor on high and keep blending until the hummus is smooth.

I kept tasting and adding more salt and more garlic powder as I went along. If you have fresh garlic cloves, use one whole glove for a fresh garlicky taste. All I had was garlic powder.

> **NOTES**
>
> You can get creative by adding roasted garlic cloves, caramelized onions, and avocado. I serve up the hummus like a condiment and if I eat it like a dip, I skip crackers and use cucumber slices.
>
> Though garbanzo beans are low-oxalate, other beans are still high. The highest of the legumes are: black beans, cannellini, adzuki beans, pinto, and soybeans.

Mango Fruit Leather

I wish I had this recipe for my kids when they were little and always looking for a snack!

This is so good, so easy, and a great little treat that is naturally sweet and can be made with fresh or frozen mango.

Get out these tools: knife, cutting board, blender, parchment paper, cookie sheet

3 cups chopped mango (I used organic, frozen mango chunks, defrosted)
juice from ½ lemon

Preheat oven to 200°F. Puree mango chunks and lemon juice in a blender until completely smooth. On a parchment lined cookie sheet, spread mango puree evenly with a spatula.

Bake for 3 to 4 hours at 200°F, until mango is firm and leathery.

When the mango is cool, cut into strips with pizza cutter or kitchen scissors.

NOTE

Use this same recipe for different fruits. Some low-oxalate options are apricots, cherry, peaches, watermelon.

Dried Apple Chips

I always see bags of these at the store, but there's added white sugar, which I do not want in my food. Making a tray of these is a better option. I love apples and enjoy them in any form: baked, raw, in a pie, applesauce, chips.

Get out these tools: knife, cutting board, cookie sheet, parchment paper

½ tsp nutmeg (or mace)
1 tbsp coconut sugar
2 Granny Smith apples, washed and sliced thin

Preheat oven to 225°F. Mix nutmeg and coconut sugar together in a small bowl.

On a parchment-paper-lined cookie sheet, place thinly sliced apple pieces and sprinkle with nutmeg and sugar.

Bake for 2 hours in 225°F oven; turn over every 30 minutes so the chips bake evenly and get crispy.

NOTES

I like these as a snack or in my No-Grain Granola. You can double or triple the recipe since the apple chips will shrink considerably while they cook—like Shrinky Dinks, remember those?

It's not hard to eat the whole pan of them when they come out of the oven. I like to make a lot of these and add to my granola.

Raw White Chocolate

3-4 servings

I've never had a really big sweet tooth, but tell me I can't have something and of course I will suddenly crave it. Chocolate is high in oxalates, and I've been both avoiding and craving it. I want a little something kind of sweet once in a while. And by once in a while, I mean every day. Just a bite. Nothing too sugary.

I discovered the joys of using cacao butter and now this is my daily treat. I buy organic Terrasoul Superfoods organic cacao butter, it melts nicely and works well to make this "raw chocolate" which is nothing like chocolate but a treat nonetheless.

Get out these tools: saucepan, whisk, wooden spoon

10–20 drops of stevia extract or 1 tbsp of raw honey
¼ cup coconut oil
1 cup cacao butter
2 tbsp coconut butter/manna
2 tsp vanilla extract
¼ tsp sea salt, optional

Add all ingredients in a saucepan and cook on low heat, stirring until all ingredients are melted. Remove from heat and pour into shallow dish. Let cool.

When it's room temperature, place in fridge to finish firming. Cut or break into pieces and store in a ziplock bag.

NOTES

Skip the vanilla and add peppermint extract, if you want a minty flavor. You can adjust the sweetness by increasing the stevia extract or raw honey. I have also used coconut sugar in this recipe and noticed the sugar will sink to the bottom of the chocolate as it cools; I don't mind because it's like a little crust.

Lately when I make this I don't use anything to sweeten it and it's still delicious. When I get around to it, I plan on buying chocolate extract and trying that out.

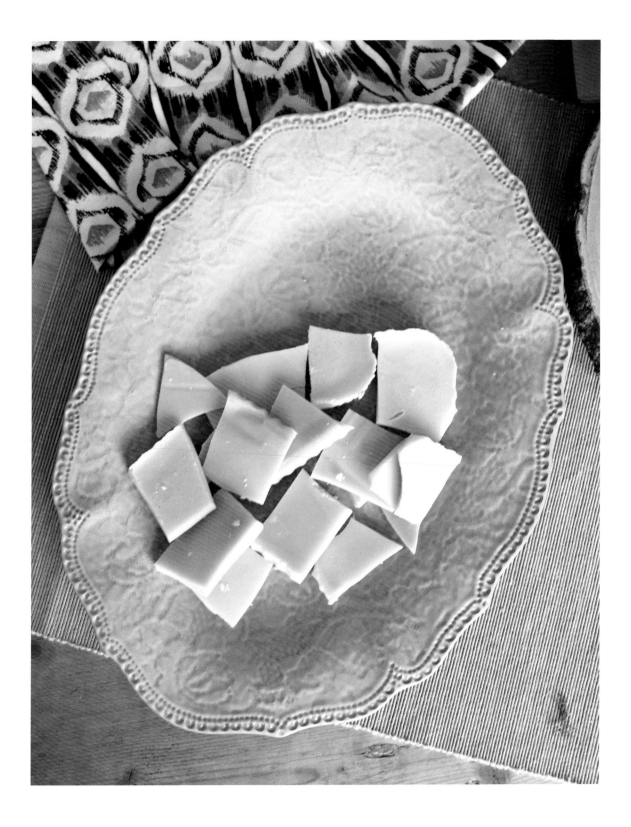

Easy Applesauce

I remember my grandmother making applesauce in her small warm kitchen. She used McIntosh apples, cinnamon, plus lots and lots of sugar, and then pureed it into a delicious sweetness that she served with pot roast and mashed potatoes. I cannot make applesauce without thinking of her.

This applesauce is low in sugar and is so good served warm. You can keep it chunky or puree into a smoother texture.

Get out these tools: knife, cutting board, saucepan, potato masher, Immersion blender

3 McIntosh apples (or Granny Smith)
4 cups of water
juice from one small lemon
¼ tsp nutmeg or if tolerated, or ½ tsp cinnamon extract
10 drops of stevia extract or ¼ cup coconut sugar

Chop apples into chunks. Boil water in saucepan, then add apples. Simmer for 25 minutes until apples are soft.

Drain water and add spices/stevia and juice from the lemon. Mash with potato masher for chunky sauce or use blender for smooth applesauce.

NOTE

I also like to make this with a little maple syrup. The maple and apple pair really well together.

Honey Vanilla Almond Coffee

1 serving

Almonds are very high in oxalates, and I avoid them at all costs for this reason alone. I am almost embarrassed to tell you how many almonds I used to consume. Tons.

Almonds are totally off the table, but we can, however, use almond extract for flavoring. I don't get fancy drinks at coffee shops because of the threat of cross-contamination with gluten as well as the very inflammatory high sugar in the drinks.

But, if time allows, I like to make this coffee drink, which is not nearly as sweet and more pure than something you may order in a coffee shop.

Get out these tools: blender, saucepan

6–8 oz. brewed coffee, room temperature
½ tsp almond extract
½ tsp vanilla extract
1½ cup of coconut milk
3 tsp raw organic honey

In a blender, add all ingredients and blend thoroughly. If you want your drink hot, heat in a saucepan over the stove.

I LOVE whipped cream and to make this drink extra fancy, I whip up a batch of fresh whipped cream. I skipped the sugar but if you like it sweet, add ten drops (more or less) of stevia extract.

Whipped Cream Topping:

1½ cups heavy whipping cream (I often use coconut cream or coconut whipping cream)
1 tsp vanilla extract

In a KitchenAid mixer or with beaters, pour whipping cream into a bowl and add extract. Beat on high until cream is thick, this takes several minutes.

Add a generous dollop to the coffee. Sprinkle with vanilla bean powder.

Whipped Vanilla Butter

makes enough for 4-5 crepes

This is so tasty on banana bread, crepes, or muffins. I paired this with my crepes and peach filling and it was a big hit!

Get out these tools: mixing bowl, beaters, spatula

3 tbsp of softened butter
1 tbsp coconut milk
1 tbsp raw honey
½ tsp vanilla★ powder.

In a mixing bowl, use beaters to thoroughly mix all ingredients until fluffy and well combined.

NOTES

Add more honey or stevia drops if you want this butter sweeter than what I have here. Always feel free to experiment and adjust the sweetness level!

*I use the Bulletproof Vanilla Powder, which has no additives, just pure vanilla beans ground into a powder.

PART THREE

Helpful Info

I've had many people asking for help with meal planning. When you are trying to follow a specific way of eating like low-oxalate, it's a challenge to come up with meals for the whole family every day that adhere to low oxalates plus gluten-free, nut-free, as well as yeast- and soy-free. That's a lot of parameters on meals and it can be overwhelming. Because I am the only one in my family who is gluten-free, yeast-free, soy-free, low-oxalate, I have to figure out what I can eat while satisfying my family's hunger too.

I like well-rounded dinners that offer lots of nutrients, mainly from various vegetables and fruits.

My general guideline is to have a protein with a vegetable with a salad. If we have dessert, it's usually fruit. If you can safely eat gluten-free pasta or rice, those are easy side dishes that everyone typically enjoys.

Here's a one-week plan for dinners pairing a main course with a side.

ONE-WEEK DINNER MEAL PLAN

DAY ONE: MEATBALLS AND ZOODLES

Meatballs made with grass-fed beef, served over Zucchini Noodles (Zoodles). I serve the homemade tomato sauce but to keep things low-ox, you can substitute the red pepper sauce.

Make it this more filling, add garlic bread or rolls. I spread butter or olive oil on bread then sprinkle with garlic powder, toast until browned.

DAY TWO: CAULIFLOWER SOUP

A simple green salad goes nicely with this soup, so do popovers which are best right out of the oven when they are warm.

DAY THREE: GREEK SALAD

Make a huge salad with romaine lettuce and other low-oxalate vegetables, feta cheese, and chicken. Serve with hummus and cucumber slices. Add chicken to make it more filling.

DAY FOUR: CHICKEN CASSEROLE

This is a one-pan dinner! You've got chicken, rice, broccoli, and cheese all baked together. Nothing else is needed, although a green salad works as a side dish with everything.

DAY FIVE: MEATLOAF

One of my favorites, meatloaf with homemade onion rings and a vegetable. I like the green beans and bacon, the flavors work so well together that my mouth is watering just thinking about it. Sautéed zucchini or cauliflower are lower oxalate options.

DAY SIX: BRAISED KIELBASA

Serve this over cauliflower or white rice. Kielbasa is high in histamines so I eat this sparingly and when I do, I enjoy every single bite.

DAY SEVEN: SHRIMP STUFFED PEPPERS

I buy the cooked, cleaned, frozen shrimp so all I have to do defrost and cook in the skillet then stuff it in halved yellow or red peppers with some rice and seasoning.

Sources and Reading

Best source of oxalate information and food lists:
http://www.lowoxalate.info/

Great overview of oxalates and information:
http://alwayswellwithin.com/2010/04/30/the-low-oxalate-diet/

In-depth look at oxalates and chronic disease
http://bioindividualnutrition.com/oxalates-their-influence-on-chronic-disease/

Informative interview with Dr. William Shaw, founder of Great Plains Labs
https://myersdetox.com/123-how-oxalates-ruin-your-health-with-dr-william-shaw/

Excellent information about oxalates, autism, and chronic disease
https://www.westonaprice.org/health-topics/vegetarianism-and-plant-foods/the-role-of-oxalates-in-autism-and-chronic-disorders/

Oxalates and autism
https://www.greatplainslaboratory.com/articles-1/2015/11/13/oxalates-control-is-a-major-new-factor-in-autism-therapy

Easy-to-understand breakdown of oxalates and oxalate issues
http://www.methylationsupport.com/wp-content/uploads/2015/04/Oxalate-and-Disease-2015.pdf

Strange symptoms and oxalates
http://blog.grasslandbeef.com/what-is-a-low-oxalate-diet-and-how-can-it-heal-your-strange-symptoms

Information about MTHFR and oxalates
http://www.beyondmthfr.com/oxalates-and-mthfr-understanding-the-gut-kidney-axis/

Overall oxalates and high-oxalate foods
https://drjockers.com/low-oxalate-diet/

Turmeric and oxalates
https://nutritionfacts.org/2015/02/12/who-should-be-careful-about-curcumin/

Quercetin as a supplement
https://www.umm.edu/health/medical/altmed/supplement/quercetin

Mangosteen helps with histamines
https://www.thealternativedaily.com/use-mangosteen-to-help-with-histamine-intolerance/

Supplements

I am sharing what has helped me. Since there is no one-size-fits-all plan or vitamin, I advise you to do your own research and talk with your medical/nutrition expert before adding anything into your diet.

- Nephure, enzyme for oxalates, https://www.nephure.com/
- Umbrellex DAO for histamine, https://www.umbrelluxdao.com/
- Mangosteen for histamine
- Quercetin for histamine
- Calcium/Magnesium supplement

Apps for Oxalates

I have two apps on my phone that I use:

- OxaBrow
- Oxalator

They both help determine which foods are high/low-oxalate and they are very useful while grocery shopping or for a quick reference.

Lab for Testing

The lab I used for histamine and pyroluria testing is DHA Laboratory https://www.dhalab.com/

Shopping

I shop a lot at Sprouts and Trader Joe's

Sprouts has locations in Alabama, Arizona, California, Colorado, Florida, Georgia, Kansas, Missouri, New Mexico, Nevada, North Carolina, Oklahoma, Tennessee, Texas and Utah.

https://www.sprouts.com/

Trader Joe's has locations across the USA.

https://www.traderjoes.com/

There is not a **Whole Foods** near my home, but I seek them out when I am traveling so I can stock up on snacks, low-oxalate produce, and supplements I may have forgotten. The salad bar is always excellent option when I can't find a restaurant with gluten-free options.

http://www.wholefoodsmarket.com/

This book was written for informational purposes only. Please consult with a qualified doctor, health coach, or dietician before making any changes to your health treatment plan or diet. Please do not attempt a low-oxalate diet without the close supervision of a health care practitioner.

Index

Index

CONVERSION CHARTS

METRIC AND IMPERIAL CONVERSIONS
(These conversions are rounded for convenience)

Ingredient	Cups/Tablespoons/ Teaspoons	Ounces	Grams/Milliliters
Butter	1 cup = 16 tablespoons = 2 sticks	8 ounces	230 grams
Cheese, shredded	1 cup	4 ounces	110 grams
Cream cheese	1 tablespoon	0.5 ounce	14.5 grams
Cornstarch	1 tablespoon	0.3 ounce	8 grams
Flour, all-purpose	1 cup/1 tablespoon	4.5 ounces/0.3 ounce	125 grams/8 grams
Flour, whole wheat	1 cup	4 ounces	120 grams
Fruit, dried	1 cup	4 ounces	120 grams
Fruits or veggies, chopped	1 cup	5 to 7 ounces	145 to 200 grams
Fruits or veggies, pureed	1 cup	8.5 ounces	245 grams
Honey, maple syrup, or corn syrup	1 tablespoon	0.75 ounce	20 grams
Liquids: cream, milk, water, or juice	1 cup	8 fluid ounces	240 milliliters
Oats	1 cup	5.5 ounces	150 grams
Salt	1 teaspoon	0.2 ounce	6 grams
Spices: cinnamon, cloves, ginger, or nutmeg (ground)	1 teaspoon	0.2 ounce	5 milliliters
Sugar, brown, firmly packed	1 cup	7 ounces	200 grams
Sugar, white	1 cup/1 tablespoon	7 ounces/0.5 ounce	200 grams/12.5 grams
Vanilla extract	1 teaspoon	0.2 ounce	4 grams

OVEN TEMPERATURES

Fahrenheit	Celsius	Gas Mark
225°	110°	¼
250°	120°	½
275°	140°	1
300°	150°	2
325°	160°	3
350°	180°	4
375°	190°	5
400°	200°	6
425°	220°	7
450°	230°	8